LOVE
SIDE BY SIDE

PARTHA SARTHI SEN SHARMA

AF118948

RUPA

Published by
Rupa Publications India Pvt. Ltd 2015
7/16, Ansari Road, Daryaganj
New Delhi 110002

Sales centres:
Allahabad Bengaluru Chennai
Hyderabad Jaipur Kathmandu
Kolkata Mumbai

Copyright © Partha Sarthi Sen Sharma 2015

This is a work of fiction. Names, characters, places and incidents are
either the product of the author's imagination or are used fictitiously,
and any resemblance to any actual persons, living or dead, events or
locales is entirely coincidental.

ISBN: 978-81-291-3765-4

Second impression 2016

10 9 8 7 6 5 4 3 2

The moral right of the author has been asserted.

Typeset by SÜRYA, New Delhi

Printed at HT Media Ltd., Noida

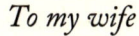

To my wife

1

Not too many people had come to college this early. There was still some half an hour left for the first classes, when the college campus would start humming with students and professors rushing, greetings, and laughter. But at eight in the morning, all was quiet, and only a few students like me were hanging around the old brick-walled playground. The 'University special' bus that took me to college was actually catering for north campus and as such, always deposited me at the gate of my engineering college well before my college would start. I could hardly recognize any of the few students sitting here and there on the red brick wall, invariably in front of their own departmental blocks, as if attached to their departments by some invisible umbilical cord. A few of them were mugging up notes in anticipation of their weekly tests.

On some days, I would be the first person to reach college and then one had to be really careful of the hordes of monkeys that infest the entire north-central Delhi. But today it was relatively safer because a few students had already arrived. Just across the main street, outside my college campus, stood Riya's college. But she would, of course, reach her college just in time, in her chauffeur-driven car like most of her fellow students of IMT. So it was no use venturing into her college at this hour. Even going to meet my hostel friends—Ravi, Joydeep, and the rest of the gang was not an option. They would invariably be rushing around, getting ready, towels wrapped around their torsos, toothbrushes in their mouths, and trying to procure optimum time in the common bathrooms and toilets.

I wanted to miss the first class and go over to IMT to meet Riya. But there is always a difference between what one wants to do and what one is expected to do. Maybe, I thought, I would go to her college during one of the ten minutes breaks and try my luck.

'Hi.' It was Rajesh, one of the many Rajeshs in my class of Mechanical Engineering, from Sarojini Nagar in South Delhi. He was dressed in his usual tailor-made, baggy trousers, a cotton printed shirt which had sleeves upto his wrists, and black, Bata leather shoes. Rajesh's father worked as a section officer in one of the many ministries of the huge monolith called the Government of India. Almost entire mini-cities like Sarojini Nagar and R. K. Puram had been set up and populated by the government in the decades immediately succeeding independence, to house its army of civil servants and clerks, during times when the government was still believed to be working for the country and its citizens' benefits.

'Hello,' I replied with a handshake. 'You are early today.'

'Yes, I got a lift. The first class is RAC's, isn't it?'

Rajesh was a very good and diligent student from a government school, quite like me, who had got admission to our prestigious government engineering college solely on the basis of the marks that he had got in class XII boards examinations. This was before every engineering college worth its name had started having an entrance exam of its own, turning the colleges wealthy and the students miserable. The fees of our government engineering college was such that Rajesh's all four brothers could study there, and secure their future without their father having to worry about fees and education loans.

Some other students had started arriving and soon we were in our cavernous lecture room with its dusty desks and tables. None of us expected that some class four staff would dust and clean the desks before the classes and neither did any any of us care. Professor Khurana would be teaching us the concepts of refrigeration that day, as he had been doing, for umpteen years before us, and would continue to do so for years till his eventual retirement. He was a sincere teacher, who regularly taught students with effort and dedication, but was not sincere enough as an academician to contribute papers to journals and magazines. I wondered if he even thought that publishing papers or conducting studies were part of his duty. After the usual wasting five minutes that were consumed by taking attendance in each class, the lecture started—totally monologous and hardly with any questions or discussions to interrupt. My fellow students were attentive enough and their degree of attention was somehow related to the economic background of their families. The class consisted of students belonging to various different socio-economic classes. Some belonged to rich business houses, who had posh houses and came to college in cars. Many of them were excellent in studies and quite intelligent, but didn't consider acquiring a graduation degree or a job during campus recruitments as their ultimate aim in life. Some of them were already thinking of joining their family business or starting on their own one. Still others used to mug up English vocabulary to clear GRE/CAT exams, either to migrate abroad or to do a MBA from any of the IIMs to embark on a career of corporate management.

Other students, the majority in fact, like Rajesh and me, belonged to ordinary middle-class families. We had joined the college to get jobs after graduation. Most of us could not afford the fees for post-graduation without scholarships, and the burden of family expectations ensured that our ambitions and foresight didn't go beyond the immediate goals. 'We' normally wore tailor-made shirts and trousers, which in Indian cheap labour market, didn't actually mean top brow luxury, and Bata shoes and concentrated on our classes and exams. We didn't want to top exactly, but were hell of a lot frightened by that prospect of 'supply'—the process of failing in one subject in the semester exams and to reappear for it six months later. 'Supply' was like an unthinkable crime, a frightening blemish for us. And then there were the hosteliers, a group within the group. They had come from all over India and were distinct from the Delhi 'day schis'—short for day scholars. The day scholars and the hosteliers were friendly towards one another but formed two distinct nations, self-contained within themselves.

2

After two classes, we—I, Rajesh, Rajeev and Prashant—
were sitting in our college canteen, sipping tea from cheap
china cups and generally chatting when Riya entered our
mournful, damp canteen with a flourish and made every
head turn around, or so I thought. True to her nature, she
never gave a damn about what others thought or talked
about her. She wore branded and imported clothes at a
time when these were not seen in Indian shops. She would
even blow kisses from the canteen gates when kisses were a
big no—even in Bombay movies. She was wearing a beige-
coloured knee length skirt and a white top, matching her
hair band, which kept her shoulder-length wavy hair in
some semblance of order.

Riya had already bought two tickets of the afternoon
show of 'Pretty Woman' and was telling me to hurry so as
not to miss the film.

'C'mon, the movie starts at three and it would take at
least an hour to reach Chanakya, even if we take an auto. I
don't want to miss even a single shot of Richard Gere,' she
said.

'But, I have classes and I can't miss them,' I protested
half-heartedly, but immensely pleased nevertheless by the
turn of events.

It was typical of her. She knew without any prior discussion that I would love the Julia Roberts–Richard Gere starrer and that was enough for her to buy the tickets in advance, regardless of whether I was ready to miss my afternoon classes or not. Of course both of us knew each other's timetables better than our own. Unlike me, classes and professors were not sacrosanct for her in themselves. They were important only to the point that they helped her achieve her exam results.

Although I felt a lurking guilt in missing my classes, the fun idea of going to a 'date' on a matinee show and the pride of doing something which my friends could not, was too much to resist. After all what is love but the irresistible desire to be irresistibly desired?

'Hey, we would get late. You can easily give up your afternoon workshop classes and I have already bought the tickets!' Riya exclaimed as if she needed to plead her case. So I waved my envious friends goodbye and we were soon sitting in an auto rickshaw on our way to Chanakya cinema—the posh south Delhi movie hall which used to screen English movies exclusively. Riya's chauffer was under instructions to drop her at her college gates and then pick her up at four in the evening, but of course, on many days, she would reach home before that, either taking a lift on one of her friend's vehicles or hiring an auto rickshaw. She rarely used a DTC bus and that would be mostly to give me company.

It was a rainy Delhi monsoon day and our black and yellow auto rickshaw moved through the heart of Delhi, through ITO and India Gate to eventually reach Chanakyapuri—diplomatic hub of New Delhi. Chanakya cinema, with its grey, brooding exteriors, stood next to the even gloomier Hotel Akbar—a government-owned hotel—and some other office blocks. The only other happening place was the newly-opened Nirula's—the trendiest place for eating and hanging out for Delhites before international food chains like Mac Donald's and KFC had been allowed entry to the hungry, Indian middle-class bellies.

The movie was beautiful and was better by the handsome lead actor and actress, the fairy tale plot, and the romantic music. It was one of those films which makes one start believing in everything good and beautiful in this world. It was emotional, yet not mushy. I bought some popcorn in the intermission as I was already feeling a bit guilty about Riya having bought the tickets. Even in the darkness of the movie hall, my timidity ensured that all our touching was limited to entwined fingers and touching knees. Kissing and necking were something that would have to wait for more private occasions. By the time Richard Gere was trying desperately to climb the ladder to Julia Robert's apartment, Riya, along with all other women in the audience, was searching for her handkerchief and all the men, including me, were waiting for the credit titles. Nevertheless, it was a 'feel good' movie and we felt good, walking along the lonely, yet busy traffic on Africa Avenue after the movie. The rain had stopped by then and it was one of those evenings when the air was moisture-laden, the sunlight was still there, and there was a peculiar quality to the light which makes everything romantic and golden.

3

I had met Riya when I had been barely eighteen. I was in my first year of engineering college and in addition to that, I was teaching school students in the evenings to get some pocket money, which made my life somewhat easier without burdening my schedule too much. I was reputed, in my neighbourhood, to be a brilliant student because of the marks in my board exams and there was no shortage of tuition offers from parents of kids who were, because of many reasons, not as adept in scoring marks as me. Most of my students were remarkably talented in some field or the other, but had some problems, especially in mathematics, the subject I knew best. Riya's younger brother, Mohit, was one of them and that is how I was introduced to Riya, although I had known of her for sometime. Our homes were in the same neighbourhood.

I don't exactly remember the day or date I first met Riya. So, I guess, it must not have been the so-called 'love at first sight'. But of course, I could see my new protégé's elder sister was not only exceptionally pretty but also, because of some unfathomable reason, unusually attentive to me. I could not then and or later decipher, why Riya liked me. She never cared to explain whenever I asked her. Maybe, she didn't know herself.

I came to know that Riya too was studying in the first semester of engineering just like me, but in Computer Science and not Mechanical Engineering. Her engineering college was new and privately run and was next to my more traditional, and government-run University. She had passed out from a prestigious private school in New Delhi with reasonably respectable, if not spectacular, marks in her exams and had secured her admission into the computer science course in the so-called 'NRI quota'. During those early days, our meetings and conversations were short and far between, and were invariably in the presence of her brother, and my student.

'Hi. How is Mohit coping up with his maths?' she had asked.

'He is doing okay, but I would prefer it if he gives some more time and attention to his studies.'

'And how is your college going?'

'Fine. The classes have just started, but the work load is yet to increase. What about you?' I had enquired.

'It is alright. Have some tea and biscuits?' she suggested, smiled, and gave way to me to start my tuitions.

Riya's parents were working in her father's company and would be out on their official engagements when I would reach their home for my classes in the evening. Although there were always at least two servants in the house, most often, it was Riya herself who opened the door to welcome me in with a smile, which was never shy. Her effervescent 'Hi' was met by my equally self-conscious 'Hello' as she led me to their study—a room which was shared by both siblings. Sometimes, Riya would continue to sit there, finishing her assignments or studying while I taught her younger brother. Our conversations would invariably take place during the tea break when she used to make it a point to bring the tray herself and share the contents as well as the conversation.

Initially the subjects of such conversations were limited to studies and happenings in our respective colleges. Since we shared the same syllabus, during our first semester, we forged conversations on our common studies. Sometimes, she would even ask me to explain certain concepts, especially in mathematics, as she had no qualms about accepting that although we were from the same batch, I was far superior in studies than her. I liked her honesty and straight-forwardness in such matters. In fact, apart from her looks, her effervescence, and straight on-your-face honesty attracted me to her, gradually as we kept meeting over the months.

One winter morning, I remember, she was wearing a pearl-white mohair sweater and a blue denim skirt. She served, along with the usual tea, a strange-looking sweet that I had not seen before.

'It is called Baklava. Papa brought it from his trip to Turkey. It is kind of famous in those regions. Do you like it? Mamma had asked me especially to serve you these,' Riya said.

I was not so daft as not to recognize that her mother would hardly care about her son's tutor so much, and that it was only Riya who wanted to share these fancy exotic delicacies with me without making me self-conscious about her charity and care. It is quite funny how our memories decide to remember such small inconsequential incidents from distant past.

I don't remember how one thing led to another, but soon we were taking time out from our respective colleges and frequenting the canteen of the neighbouring one. I remember my first birthday after I had met her. We never used to celebrate my birthday at home in the usual fashion and it was therefore doubly surprising and pleasant for me to find out that Riya had actually taken care to remember my birthday. She had taken time and effort to even buy me a gift and a greeting card. The words on that first birthday card that I ever received were sort of neutral and non-committal. It hinted at care and friendship without actually professing anything. The words on that card spoke less than what she wanted to say, but more than I dared to imagine.

I had not met too many girls during my school days although I had studied in a co-ed school. For one, I was too young and too preoccupied with my studies to think about the girls in my school, pretty as some of them were. So, Riya was, in many ways, the first non-familial member of the opposite sex with whom I had had any chance to come in contact. I had never expected to share someone like Riya's company, and soon her smiles, her attention and her nature had me smitten. Even before it had been six months since I had met her, I was in love, or so I believed!

4

Believing that I was in love was one thing, but professing it openly was entirely different. So, many months passed before we sort of accepted that there was something going on between us and by that time there was no longer any need to profess anything. It was clear even to a blind person who saw us together.

But those months when we sort of pretended to one another, to our common friends, and sometimes even to ourselves that we were just 'good friends' was real fun. We both knew and understood that there was something special—some special chemistry—between us but were not sure that it was 'love'. To be sure that one is in love is damn difficult as the concept of love itself is so nebulous, amorphous, and multi-faceted. But apart from that, I was afraid—of being rejected and even worse, laughed at, by this effervescent and bubbly girl. Riya used to joke and pull my leg so much in those initial months—partly to make an excuse to prolong our conversations—that I was not sure, or rather I was afraid to be sure, whether she felt something special for me.

So months passed and we remained very good friends without graduating to the next level. Initially, we went out for movies and lunches, accompanied by some of our common friends as a meal or movie between just the two of us was a sort of acceptance or declaration that we were more than just friends. But slowly, and again, I don't remember when was the first time, but we started going to movies and meals, always lunch, unaccompanied by our friends. As I used to take private tuitions in the evenings, I had some reasonable amount of cash with me. Therefore going to movies in Chanakya or Priya or for meals at Chopsticks or Essex Farms, once in a while, was no big deal.

If one were to believe in Hindi movies—which every Indian would like to but does not actually believe in—it would appear that a love story between a boy and a girl is a 'done' thing and has always been so, right from the days when the talkies arrived in 1930s. But love stories in Indian college campuses are not as common, especially in north India, as one would like it to be. And especially, in engineering colleges, where the number of girls is always extremely low, such love stories are even rarer. So slowly, I and Riya, and our relationship became sort of well-known in both our campuses—not in a negative sort of way, but more in curious and even envious kind. Of course, Riya didn't give two hoots about what others talked or thought about her. She was true and carefree, and couldn't be bothered by other peoples' reactions. As for me, I was secretly happy and proud that my college mates regarded me and Riya to be in some sort of special relationship. It was an acceptance of the fact that I could be considered good enough for her, and that was a great ego booster for me in those days!

5

It was not that my life was totally one-dimensional, that it revolved around Riya, and that there was nothing else in my life. Of course, I had my parents, my selflessly adoring Indian mother, my distant yet supportive father, my sister, and my friends, both in college and neighbourhood. But Riya and studies did become the two most important and consuming issues for me, in those days.

I remember, once during one of our semester breaks, I and a couple of my college friends—Rajesh and Prashant—had decided to take a break and travel to Himachal Pradesh. Prashant belonged to a small and remote village in the Kangra district of the state. His father used to work in Air India and he had many paternal relatives living in Kangra. His uncles from mother's side lived in the adjoining district of Chamba. It was the very first time that I was taking a journey without my parents and as such it was quite an adventure with its thrill of the unknown. I suspect it might have been the same for Prashant and Rajesh too, although none of us would admit it, at that time, to the others. We boarded an overnight train from the New Delhi Railway station to Pathankot from where we were to travel by bus to Kangra. Autumn was merging into winter, and the cold air rushing in through the window shutters of the second class railway carriage, was biting. Although the platform was full of uniformed army men, the surroundings of the Pathankot Railway station that morning resembled that of every other north Indian railway station—dirty, dark eateries waking up from inadequate slumber, cycle rickshaws and auto rickshaws jostling for space amidst honking buses, hordes of villagers coming to the city for the first time, and gawking at the semi-nude females from B-grade Hindi film posters. We found a place to eat and due to some strange reason ended up ordering dosas—a typically south Indian dish—sitting in the heart of the Punjab. Predictably, the dosas ended up tasting like something between the real thing and paranthas.

The bus journey from Pathankot to Kangra was quite delightful, and Prashant's relatives both at Kangra and later at Chamba, were very humble and genuinely welcomed the sudden intrusion of their nephew's friends. We were, in fact, treated as some sort of celebrities, as we were educated, urban and more importantly could speak English, which sounded sufficiently fluent to their unaccustomed ears.

It is rather strange that all sorts of otherwise unremarkable things and ordinary events stick to our memories and many other more traditionally important things are forgotten. So I would have liked to remember the ruins of the Kangra fort or the miniature 'Pahari' paintings in the museum or the ancient Devi temple at Chamba but what I actually remember is drinking beer in the dimly lit 'Ravi View Café'—with the murmur of the almost invisible River Ravi flowing from its deep, dark valley. This was the first time I heard about a sixteen-year-old boy, who had not only made to the Indian test team touring Pakistan, but was also clobbering their ace leg spinner for consecutive sixes with confidence verging on arrogance. Although that particular series belonged to the more sedate Sanjay Manjrekar, the son of his illustrious father, but that sixteen-year-old boy was to become Sachin Tendulkar—a name which has since then accompanied me through the ups and downs of life, year after year, and has probably contributed more to the gross domestic happiness of this country than any other single individual in all these years.

Those were the days when there were no mobile phones, and even landline telephones were not to be found in ordinary middle class Indian homes. So, although I was enjoying my first independent trip away from home with my friends, sometimes, I used to miss Riya, especially when I was alone or just before falling asleep. In fact, that was probably the first time I realized for sure that I was indeed in love with her.

6

We grew up on a staple overdose of Hindi films and English novels, both of which led us to believe in the concept of eternal romantic love. Love was, by its very definition, eternal and if not beyond life then at least, once in a lifetime. And so naturally, I started believing that Riya was the person, meant for me and there was absolutely no doubt in my mind that I would always love her, and her only. One thing led to another and I had decided, before I had reached the age of twenty, on my choice of life partner, even before asking her thoughts on this matter. Only the practical and therefore, mundane things like graduation, the possibility of higher education, getting a job and earning a livelihood, and the acceptance of families lay before me and realizing my dream. Regardless of whatever may happen in future, I felt totally committed to a life time spent with Riya, since I believed that I loved her.

On her part, Riya did nothing to discourage my faith and it was clear not only to me and to our mutual friends that not only she did like me, she was also exceptionally fond of me, and loved spending her spare time with me, much to the chagrin of her friends and hopeful suitors. She was extremely comfortable with the idea of going against expected conventions to please me, and didn't give it a second thought.

We were in our fifth semesters when one of Riya's many college friends, Harpreet, a rich bloke, threw his birthday bash in a posh south Delhi club and invited me too, out of a sense of courtesy or rather to ensure that Riya did not decline the invitation. There were drinks and a dance floor, and although Riya was a natural dancer and loved to dance, she made it a point that evening not to step on the dance floor even once, since I was too self-conscious to dance in those days. I did act to encourage her to dance, and there were no shortage of willing partners but Riya spent the entire evening with me. We kept sitting in a darkish corner throughout the evening, sipping slowly at our drinks and looking at the dancers gyrating or making fools of themselves to the beats of loud western music. Michael Jackson's 'Bad' was the rage that year and attempts at moonwalking were common ways to show off. Although, I liked to believe that I was not possessive about my love, but it made me feel gratified about Riya's gesture.

It was late in the night, on our way back home, when I asked her. 'Why didn't you dance today? All your friends must have been so disappointed.' Although it was the height of summer, the breeze made the night cool and comfortable. The branches of huge gulmohur trees, lining the street, swayed in the breeze, casting their dancing shadows on the footpath.

'So what? I don't dance for them. I dance for myself, and tonight I didn't feel like it. That's all,' Riya replied shrugging, looking straight ahead.

'But they would think that I am the spoil sport,' I mentioned.

'Why do you think about what others think?' Riya queried.

There was no answer to that question. My upbringing had programmed my brain to think in a particular way and hers had programmed her to work in a particular fashion.

I could never figure out why Riya seemed to like me so much. It seemed such a fragile 'fact' that I didn't dare to venture to ask her about it lest she should deny it altogether. I loved to imagine, and felt more and more convinced that she too loved me, whether she admitted it to herself or not. Anyhow, all circumstantial evidence supported my optimistic thesis.

7

Strange though it may seem, nevertheless it is true that neither do I remember the first time I openly professed my love to Riya, in words, in person, nor her reaction. But by and by, as we moved from semester to semester, from exams to exams, and from birthdays to birthdays, we reached a stage when it was taken for granted by both of us that we were destined to live our lives together. It was not so much as spoken promises, or professing of our eternal romantic love, or anything of that sort but by our third year in college, or rather sixth semester, when I believed the time had come for me to declare my, or our, intentions to her, and our parents.

I had always been a sort of straightforward person and considered concealment or deceit acts of cowardice. I didn't feel I was in any way on the wrong path and further, I felt that it was my moral duty not to keep my parents, and more importantly her parents in the dark any longer. They had put their faith in me.

When I broached the subject to my mother, she seemed to be totally nonchalant about it as though she had already known what was coming. Maybe parents, and especially mothers, have a knack of knowing and understanding, by intuition, the minds and lives of their offsprings, from their behaviour. She was neither ecstatic about it nor totally and vociferously opposed to the whole thing. Maybe, she realized that direct opposition would not yield any favourable results. She knew how independent and stubborn her only son was.

'Maa, I want to talk to you about something…something that is very important to me,' I said. We were in our kitchen. She was preparing lunch for all of us, as she did every day, throughout her married life. She didn't say anything.

'It is about Riya,' I added.

There was no answer or response from her as she busied herself in preparing the daal on the gas burner.

'We have decided to marry each other, when the time comes,' I said in our common native tongue, a language that was utterly foreign to Riya, as a matter of fact.

'Has she also decided?' she asked for the first time.

'Yes, we have both decided,' I replied.

My mother had, by that time, met Riya on a few occasions. She had not given anything away about her feelings about Riya. Riya had been her usual friendly and effervescent-self, and my mother was always polite and sincere in her behaviour.

'Do her parents know?' she asked.

'Not yet. I decided to tell you first,' I said, thinking it would please her to know that she was more important than Riya's parents. If she was pleased particularly, it didn't show, however.

'You should talk to your father,' she said as she took the daal out of the container and poured it into another serving cauldron.

'Yes, I will,' I said and moved away. I knew talking to my father would be very different and much more difficult than talking to my mother. My relationship with my father was quite distant, to say the least. I admired many of his qualities—particularly his struggle in the difficult post-partition times to educate himself and become self-reliant. I guessed he also liked and was proud of his son. But our conversations were always perfunctory and matter-of-factly, whenever they were. He didn't find it particularly easy to share his feelings and his thoughts with his offsprings. Most of the time, when we did have a talk, it was about the status of Indian cricket, a topic which warmed us both. This was actually not very abnormal or unnatural in those days, as many, if not most, of my friends had very similar relationship with their fathers. The father of the family was the great patriarch, the bread-winner, sitting on a high pedestal, not necessarily by his choice, and was not expected to share his thoughts, let alone emotions, with his children. He was trapped in his expected role and inherited image, and didn't dare break the mould to come face to face with his own offsprings.

Although my mother had asked me to tell my father, I soon discovered that she had herself shared my story with him, and in a fashion that had led to a sort of acceptance by my father. I think it was a rather difficult situation for them and they didn't know how to form their reactions to a sort of fait accompli. But overall, they didn't pose any objection at my decision and kept quiet, waiting for life to unfold. Riya and her family belonged to a different part of our vast country and there were differences of language, culture, community, and societal relations between the two families. But such inter-community marriages, especially in Indian metros, at that time, were becoming increasingly common and the old irrevocable differences were gradually giving way to homogeneity, born out of an urban, educated, middle-class milieu.

8

After I had divulged our future plans to my parents, the next natural step was to inform Riya's parents. Somehow, in my enthusiasm and boldness, I felt it was my duty and not Riya's, to tell our decision to her parents. Riya could have told her parents about how she felt about me just as I had done. But I was probably impatient. More likely, I wanted to shield her from any potential unpleasantness and displeasure of her parents and wanted to take the chivalrous responsibility for our relation.

It was a cold winter evening and I reached her house when I had no tuitions to take, knowing fully well that Riya's mother was at home and not her father. Somehow, I felt Mrs Malhotra would be more understanding. Riya had inherited her looks and her nature, as far as I could make out, from her mother. Mr Malhotra was a rather round-the-clock businessman. He ran a business that he had inherited from his father-in-law, and I suspected that he would not understand matters of heart and feelings through his money-tinted glasses. I always had more faith on women, anyway.

I wore a beige coloured jacket, the best I had, and black, neatly pressed trousers. Mrs Malhotra offered me tea and all three of us, including Riya, sat in the drawing room. It was difficult for me as my previous conversations with Mrs Malhotra, although frequent, were generally about her son's progress in mathematics. She was always polite, self-assured, and fair in her behaviour towards me. But I didn't know how long that would last after I had said what I had come to say that day.

'Aunty, I think that it is only fair for us to inform you that we, I and Riya, love each other and are quite serious about it,' I finally mustered enough courage to tell Mrs Malhotra, after some initial hesitation.

If she was shocked or angry, she didn't really express it. Mrs Malhotra, with admirable self-restraint, behaved perfectly normal and glanced towards her daughter. Riya was usually exuberant, much more than me, but on that evening, she remained silent. However, she didn't refute my contention and silently nodded in support.

I was prepared for the worst but Mrs Malhotra simply said, 'Look. I think both of you are too young to make such final decisions about your lives. It is too early to make such deep commitments.'

'Maybe so, but I am sure about my feelings and definitely want to marry Riya. I wanted to share that with you. Of course, nothing is going to happen right away and we have to finish our studies, get settled and all that. But I thought that you should know from us rather than from some third person,' I found myself saying.

The fact was that I was more than relieved by Mrs Malhotra's reactions as she had not flown off the handle, prohibiting us to meet, cancelling her son's tuitions, and driving me out of her house. I suspected that she had some clue about her daughter's feelings and therefore was averse to antagonize and provoke Riya. It was a burden off my chest as I felt I had done what was morally right—declaring my love and commitment to all concerned so that we could not be accused of deceit or breach of faith by anyone.

It was a matter of days before Riya told me that her mother had shared our conversation with Mr Malhotra and had made him see sense and inevitability. Mr Malhotra didn't broach the topic with me in our subsequent meetings and behaved well, and was favourably disposed towards me. So, I gathered he was not totally opposed to the prospect either. I didn't think her parents, or mine, could have really stopped us from meeting each other. We felt too strongly for each other and also for our independence. But they could have made our lives difficult, thrown tantrums, created scenes, and just made everything rather unpleasant. But they chose not to, and so Riya and I continued seeing each other, encouraged by the silent, if not enthusiastic, acceptance of our parents. Our relationship was now more in the open and I started to drive my newly acquired mobike, Yamaha RX 100, up to her door to take her to movies or dinners. I was happy and so was Riya.

9

Mugging up definitions of difficult English words for GRE/CAT/GMAT exams was nothing extraordinary for final year students in either of our engineering colleges. But still I was a bit surprised when Riya started carrying newly bought GRE books to college along with her usual course books. After all, GRE meant going to the USA for post graduate studies. Since I was not thinking on those lines, it would mean separation for at least two years, if not more, provided of course Riya was serious and successful in her attempt.

'Hi. Are you planning to appear for GRE exams?' I asked tentatively during one of our journeys to college. We were sitting in an auto rickshaw that was moving through the AIIMS crossing.

'Yes. What's the harm? I would be taking GMAT and TOEFL too. It is a bit early but I would probably need to appear at least twice to get a decent score,' Riya replied. I didn't know when she had decided upon GRE/GMAT but it appeared to be the natural choice to her.

'Do you intend to pursue higher studies in the USA?' I asked stupidly. Why else would anybody appear for GRE?

'Naturally. A mere B.E degree from a private engineering college in Delhi would not sustain in the long run. I think you should also seriously think of applying to USA colleges for post-graduation,' Riya replied.

'But I need to start earning early. Both for my family and for us to settle down,' I said as the auto rickshaw crossed over the Safdarjung flyover. A sports biplane was touching down on the airstrip.

'What's the hurry to settle down or to start earning? I think you should seriously think of going abroad. You are such a bright student, I am sure you would easily get admission as well as a decent scholarship,' Riya said, trying to boost my ego and mood.

No matter how much Riya tried to reason with me over the next few days to appear for GRE/GMAT/TOEFL exams and subsequently get admission into some USA university for post graduation, I remained firm. Going to the USA had not been in my original scheme of things ever. I was looking forward to getting a decent job through campus recruitment and start earning, as soon as possible. My parents wished me to start earning too as my father was due to retire from his government job, the next year. Although he was to get his pension, as all government employees got, we would have to look for alternative accommodation, and the family income would decrease. My sister was about to get admission to the university, and the recent liberalization of higher education was sure to be expensive. All this I could not explain to Riya as it seemed too obvious for her to see by herself. With all our intimacy, commitment, and love, it still hurt my ego to discuss my family's financial constraints with her. I also suspected that even if I tried, she would not understand them fully. The fact that I had decided on my choice of wife on my own, without consulting my parents, meant that I felt doubly obliged to fulfill their other expectations from me. They didn't profess any expectations from me, ever. But I could see that an additional salary would be more than welcome in our family at that stage. I knew that my father had done the same and more during his time with the explicit burden of family expectations weighing on his then young shoulders. They were three brothers and four sisters, and for some time after his graduation, he had remained almost the sole bread earner for his entire family and it was through his income that one by one, the sisters got married and the house was made 'pucca' before he himself decided to tie the knot at a relatively late age. Nobody had even hinted me to do anything remotely similar, but I felt a moral obligation to start earning as soon as possible. I wanted to get a job early, also because it would have given me the financial independence to marry Riya. But now her plans to study abroad meant that marriage might have to wait.

10

The fact that Riya had decided to apply for studying abroad, without consulting me, did hurt. Maybe, she thought that going for studies to the USA was the only natural progression available and therefore, didn't think it necessary to discuss it with me. She was, in fact, sort of taken aback on my stubborn reluctance to do the same and tried to coax me to change my decision.

'Look, no matter how brilliant a student you are, in the coming years a post graduate degree or MBA would be considered a minimum qualification for the top jobs. I don't understand why, with your aptitude, you would want to restrict yourself and your ambitions?' She was aghast. We were sitting in a new café. Coffee was fast becoming the fashionable drink for the young and educated in Indian metros.

'We can do a part-time MBA from Delhi University while working,' I countered.

'Come on. You know pretty well that it is not the same thing. A part-time degree is not the same as a "proper" MBA degree from abroad. Anyway, I cannot hope to get a decent job with my degree in India. Also, foreign education would give me, us, exposure. We would see the USA and the world,' Riya was adamant as always.

'Look, I really don't think that the guys who are studying abroad are coming back to contribute here. Their knowledge, acquired in USA colleges is hardly useful here. We work very differently,' I said.

'That is the whole problem. We don't want to learn. We want to remain frogs in our small wells,' Riya was getting angry, upset, and frustrated as she turned her face away to see the mad traffic outside through the large window panes of the café.

'Maybe, I am a frog in a well. But I really don't think that all your friends are dying to go to the USA to gain better knowledge and learn techniques, and then come back to India and apply them here. They are simply going to emigrate to the USA, get a job there, earn in dollars, get a green card and have fun,' I replied.

'So, what's wrong in having fun? What's wrong in wanting to live a decent life in a decent country? What's wrong in trying to grow and make a life for one's self? Must I live in India with its quota raj and mad democracy where nothing works?' Riya was no longer in her usual jovial mood. The Prime Minister had recently announced the implementation of the recommendations of the so-called Mandal Commission. Now there would be additional quota in jobs and government colleges for students belonging to OBCs, or 'Other Backward Castes' in addition to the already existing reservations for those belonging to Scheduled Castes and Scheduled Tribes. It was a hugely unpopular decision among the upper caste students of Delhi University, at that time.

'Who asked you to do anything of that sort? I know I cannot, and I don't intend to ask you to change any of your career plans or ambitions,' I said matter-of-factly as I asked for the bill. 'Let's go. It is getting late. Your parents would get worried.'

Although, there had been numerous occasions earlier when we had returned much later, after a dinner.

11

'So, you won't appear for the GRE and you won't go abroad for studies?' Riya asked me for the umpteenth time. We were sitting in the revolving restaurant near Connaught Place. The restaurant didn't revolve and its name 'Parikrama' was the only reminder that it did revolve for a few months, immediately after its inauguration, some ten years ago.

'You know I can't. Besides, as you know, I have already got a job with the TATA Company in my campus interview and I am looking forward to joining them,' I said.

'It is your wish and mindless stubbornness,' Riya said. 'Tell me, should I give GRE or not?' she asked.

'Of course, you should.'

I knew that Riya had already applied for the exams and they were to be held next Sunday. Her centre was at ITO.

'But, what about us?' Riya asked. She had, for the first time, broached the topic of our common future.

'Look,' I held her hands over the table and looked into her eyes. 'No relationship can last, based merely on sacrifice. You go abroad, pursue your studies, and fulfil your dreams. I know two years is a long time, especially without you, but if our love is real, we would be able to survive the separation and I would be waiting for you when you come back,' I said hoping I sounded convincing.

Riya smiled but the smile was not her usual effervescent one. She entwined her fingers in mine and said, 'I know, but I still don't understand you. We could have given GRE together, and applied for the same college. You with scholarship, and I with my papa's money. It would have been real fun. Just think of it.' She looked at me wistfully, almost pleading.

'Too good to be true. Anyway, two years is not such a long time and we are not getting too old and bald by then,' I said, trying to lighten the mood unsuccessfully.

'So when are you supposed to join the TATAs?' Riya asked, changing the topic.

'First of July. It is still some time away. Other companies are coming to our campus but I am now disqualified for appearing in other interviews as I have already got an offer. Not that I am complaining as this would be the best job,' I said.

'Yes, but maybe HLL?' She enquired. No company came for campus recruitment to her college.

'I don't want to sell soaps and toothpastes for the rest of my life,' I said, smilingly. I had learnt of this cliché a few days back. It was used to denigrate all MNC consumable product companies, whether they actually manufactured soap or not. Especially by students who never got a chance to apply for a HLL job because of the high qualifying marks demanded. I was not one of them but still it was a nice line, too good to resist.

'What's wrong in that? HLL pays twice as much as TELCO and it is a MNC,' Riya said. She had no qualms in accepting her natural desire to earn good money and to have a good life. She also had a great fascination for foreign lands, I had learnt. And by foreign lands I don't mean Africa. She was hugely impressed by the first world—the white world—as I said, by USA, England, and Europe. Maybe it was her father's influence and his talks of foreign trips and his export–import business. For her, English literature was far greater than anything Indians wrote in vernacular, Hollywood movies were far superior to Indian movies, western music was far more catchy than Hindi film numbers, and even western cuisine was better than Indian. I had great difficulty in agreeing to all these and especially to the last one.

'Anyway, the question does not arise as I have already been selected by TATAs and I'm set to join their graduate training programme on the first of July. Maybe, who knows, by that time you would be all set to go abroad,' I said. I didn't feel nice saying those words, although I tried to keep a brave, stiff upper lip expression.

'Who knows what future has in store for us?' Riya exclaimed, finishing her ice cream. I was a little startled at her last sentence. I thought we had already decided about our future.

12

The monsoons had hit the city with full force. It was green and glistening all around and even the previously dusty and infertile land was giving rise to life which no one could have suspected to be there, hidden in its sterile bosom. Riya had got admission in the New York State University and was about to fly next Friday night. Even by her parents' standards, it was going to cost a considerable sum of money for her University fees and on top of that the cost of living in New York was also much higher than the other parts of the USA. All this knowledge, of course, came to me through Riya only, as any expenditure of such was totally remote to me.

'Yes, it is initially going to be expensive but once I finish my studies, I would be able to earn many times over and so I guess, if you look at it from that angle, it is a wise investment decision,' Riya told me one rainy evening as we sat in our usual corner table in Essex Farms in South Delhi. She was having some pink coloured frothy shake and I was having my usual dark espresso.

'Yes, I am sure,' I replied.

'I wish you had decided to go to USA too,' Riya said for the umpteenth time.

'I think we have gone through this course before and anyway it is too late in the day,' I said.

I was booked on the train to Jamshedpur next Sunday, two days after Riya's eminent departure. Even after getting a job offer from the TATA, I had been offered few more jobs from respectable public sector companies like Maruti—a major automobile company located near Delhi, which was at that time, before divestment became fashionable, still very much a public sector company, and Indian Oil—the largest petroleum company in the government sector. But I had retained my original decision to join the TATAs, not only because of the timeless prestige and reputation of the group, but also because it automatically meant that I would be shifting, from Delhi to the remote city-town of Jamshedpur, thirty-six hours by train from Delhi. The prospect of living in Delhi, moving through the same streets and friend circles, without Riya was a bit too much to bear for me, or so I thought.

The Friday Riya left, I had gone to her home in the evening to meet her. She was busy and her hands and her mind were literally full with last minute packing. She was excited and a bit anxious at the same time. She had travelled abroad before, unlike me, who never had the need or the chance to even get his passport. But this was the first time she was to travel abroad alone. I had accompanied her for the previous couple of months through her ordeals with visa, insurance, medical check-ups, applications, and all the other mindless formalities that were needed and now the time had come to say goodbye. She would be away from India and me for at least a good six months, if not more. Her parents were at home and hovering over her preparations. So there had been hardly any opportunity for me that day to spend any time with Riya alone except for saying a few polite, formal platitudes, while having the customary tea in her mother's presence. I had decided not to go to the airport to see her off. For one, after midnight, there was no means of public transport in Delhi, and it would have cost so much money to hire a taxi so the idea never cropped up in my mind. Also, Riya never asked me to be at the airport to see her off. Her parents had seen her off on that Friday night and by the time I woke up the next morning, Riya was far away from my countries' boundaries, somewhere over the Atlantic Ocean. She was the first thing that came to my mind as I woke up, as was usual, and I imagined her to be thinking of me. Till date I don't know whether I was right.

13

My leaving home, for good as I realized later, was an important event in my life, as I guess it is also for others. But at that time, the event's significance was lost on me, just as it appeared to be lost on my parents. I undertook a thirty-six-hour-long train journey on the Neelanchal Express to Jamshedpur, on a second class carriage, two days after Riya left. By this time, I had already travelled a few times without my parents but never totally alone. The romance of the train journey through the vast hinterland of the country, amidst intermittent monsoon showers, and changing landscapes, was overshadowed by my feelings of desperation, emanating from Riya's absence. It was made only worse by my constant brooding on the same. Riya had become more than a habit for me, a sort of second skin by her constant presence in my life, in my times, and in my thoughts. Separation from her though was painful, but the heart didn't want to let go of it, either.

The land had turned reddish with the hidden iron, when the train carrying me snaked into the Tatanagar Railway station, the next morning, around two hours late, and around half an hour after I had woken up. As I emerged from the railway station—named after the founder member of the family empire—the first sight that greeted me, and every other passenger—was a series of auto rickshaw drivers and bus drivers. There were no taxis. The drivers were shouting at the top of their lungs—'Telco!' 'Sakchi!' 'Bishtupur!'—the various destinations that they were bound for and were advertising to their potential passengers. As my hired auto rickshaw entered the portals of the proper TATA township—after hardly a kilometre or so—the quality of the road and almost everything else improved dramatically and one got a feeling that he had entered an island of order, sense, and reason amidst the chaos, confusion, and filth of the rest of its surroundings. That 'island-ish' feeling never left me during my entire stay in Jamshedpur, although the contours of the island kept changing with time, situation, and my thoughts. I guess, the feeling would be similar while living in other similar artificial townships that have been created around large public sector factories, power plants, or mines. And despite the artificiality and superficial sterility of these islands, the oases were blessings to its residents, compared to the rest of their countrymen, though one, that many of them didn't realize.

My auto rickshaw crossed the TISCO township and localities like Sakchi and Bishtupur, which only by their names resemble the ancient tribal villages that had existed there, till they were subsumed into the modern industrial township that had grown around the steel factory almost a century ago. Although the tribals of these villages must have had lost their centuries old, traditional ways of living, their descendants working in the modern factories, admittedly mostly as labourers and in blue collar jobs, didn't appear to be unhappy. But then the entire concept of happiness is such an amorphous and nebulous one that the person himself is not clear whether he is really happy, let alone others.

The township of TELCO was situated on the other side of the city of Jamshedpur, and although more than fifty years old, was still new compared to its more ancient cousin of steel. It was to become and remain for the next three years of my youth, my hometown—so as to say—and despite my restless separation from Riya, the days were happy and pleasant, or so it seems today, across the intervening years that have the ability to make reality appear a bit different from what it was. But then who can say what is perception and what is reality or whether there exists anything distinctly real other than perception? I do remember noticing the huge concrete arch proclaiming the entrance to the TELCO township as my auto rickshaw scampered past the closed iron gates of the factory on my right, towards the bachelor trainee engineers' hostel called— what else—'Engineers' Hall,' my first in an unending series of residences away from my parents' roof.

14

Today it is indeed difficult to imagine a life without the internet and mobile phones. And if I recall those days of my youth when they didn't exist, today, a young reader would think that I am an ancient creature from a long lost world—a sort of dinosaur—and he or she wouldn't be totally inaccurate in their innocent imagination. But indeed there was no internet or mobiles during my entire stay in Jamshedpur and the only way to keep in touch with Riya, or with my family, except for the occasional call made from a public phone booth, was through letters delivered by the postal department. Of course, our imagination was not fertile enough to conjure such futuristic conveniences as the internet or mobile, and so there was no sense of deprivation. One cannot miss things one cannot imagine. And so the eagerly anticipated letters from Riya were a source of expectant joy every time one of them was delivered by the invisible postman under the closed doors of my hostel room, when I was away on my duty in the plant.

I was living away from my family, my home, and my hometown for the first time in my life, but I never felt anything like home-sick, whatever may have been the reason. Maybe I was brought up, expecting to live on my own as soon as I was finished with my education. I was living in a sparsely furnished hostel, maintained by the company, situated amidst an entire township, again created and maintained by it. It had been constructed to house the bachelor trainee engineers, who like me, were fresh out of their colleges, had arrived from all parts of India and one could see a small microcosm of our vast country. The trouble TELCO took, at least in those days, to go to distant college campuses, situated in all parts of our vast country, to offer jobs to young, inexperienced engineers was not only to attract the best of talent but also, I guess, to foster a kind of diversity in its workforce, which only now modern management gurus have come to advocate.

I am not sure how much this great diversity in recruitment helped the company as a lot of these young, talented people left the company—their first jobs—only after a couple of years, despite the best efforts of the company to retain them, but it made our lives far richer in those youthful days. So I had friends—genuine ones, and not merely colleagues, the kinds you make only in your youth—from Punjab, from the dusty moffusil towns of UP, from the industrial townships of south Bihar— Jharkhand was a mere demand and not reality then—from Calcutta, from the distant shores of Kerala, from the ancient temple towns of Tamil Nadu, from the metropolises of Delhi and Bombay, from far off Suratkal, and from Orissa. Only and maybe revealingly, although it did not reveal anything to me at that time, Kashmir, the north eastern states, and (surprisingly) Gujarat were exceptions and I don't remember any of my colleagues, having come from these states.

We were young and independent so far as our economic

conditions were concerned. We were living away from our families and pretended to be adventurous without actually being so, having arrived at Jamshedpur from our respective middle class families. As far as actual work was concerned, we undertook an almost three-month-long training in the factory itself—in its various divisions—and therefore, in the initial months at least, had no real responsibilities and concerns. Weekends were enjoyable as were the evenings, and we had more than ample time in our hands. Friends were made and lost—some to be retained over years, others to be remembered and occasionally to be regained later through Facebook accounts. We made day-long excursions on our newly-acquired bikes to nearby forests and waterfalls that surrounded the town of Jamshedpur, situated as it was amidst the green plateaus of Chota Nagpur, on the banks of the peculiarly named River Subarnarekha—which literally meant the golden line river.

15

'Hello. My name is Rajesh Kumar Singh,' said my roommate, who was one year senior to me. The Engineers Hall was strictly occupied by the company's graduate engineer trainees, called GET, for short. The period of training lasted two years, therefore at any point of time, two batches of trainees occupied the hall—one junior and the other one year senior. Rajesh belonged to the senior batch and had already lived in the hall, and in Jamshedpur for one year before I invaded his room.

'Hi. My name is Pankaj,' I introduced myself. We shook hands as is the custom in such situations, especially among men. He was from a city in northern Bihar and had studied in an engineering college there. Rajesh was shy, a rather reluctant conversationalist but a simple, straight forward and trustworthy soul with simple views and simpler needs. He was a peaceful and friendly roommate, but there were others in the hall who gradually became friendlier as conversations with Rajesh were at best, deliberate and short. He would invariably bring and share delicious litchis from his hometown during the season, as he was justifiably proud of the fame that his hometown was known for the best of these fruits in all over India. He would just dump a large bunch of these delicious fruits on my bed, in my absence, without speaking a single word.

Elderly gentlemen would come knocking on holidays, looking for Rajesh as a prospective bridegroom for their daughters, nieces, or other unmarried young female relatives. I could see that Rajesh was considered a very eligible bachelor among his community, a perfect fit as a bridegroom for a traditional arranged marriage. Naturally, all the prospective in-laws belonged to his community of Bihari Bhumihars. But Rajesh didn't get married till the end of the year that we shared our room in the hall. He was reluctant to meet fathers of prospective brides and used to go to endless troubles to avoid them without giving the impression of being rude or arrogant. It was much later that I gathered that he secretly wanted to marry the daughter of his college's principal in his hometown, whose favourite he had been. Rajesh was from a rural background and he had studied and lived, for the most part of his school days, in his native village somewhere in north Bihar, before moving to the engineering college and hostel of a mofussil city. Maybe, the differences of our respective upbringing or his naturally introvert nature never allowed our companionship to develop into real friendship, but I always respected him and have reasons to believe that he did not totally dislike me.

16

It was one of those slightly chilly late autumn mornings when the morning breeze asks one to wear something warmer over the usual summer cotton clothes, and the sun starts losing its terrible power to scorch the earth. It was a welcome holiday and I, Gautam, Puri, and Alok had decided to go on a day-long trek to the nearby Dalma forests. It took us more than an hour on our bikes and scooters to reach the solitary but popular roadside dhaba on the highway to Ranchi (a city outside Jamshedpur), where we had decided to have breakfast and park our two-wheelers safely before starting on our trek. It was more than a dhaba but less than a proper restaurant. Yet it had a beer bar license. We had come there before too and the owner knew from our looks that we were educated employee officers belonging to the TATA's stable. After a quick brunch we started our trek to the top of Dalma. Dalma was a green, forested hillside, known for hosting occasional hordes of wild elephants. The trek through the green forested hillside, with the open sky above our heads and the autumn breeze blowing like a cold breath, were pleasant and rare for a city-bred chap like me. We made our way through red-soiled hill tracks, amidst green shrubs and prickly bushes but there was not the slightest sign of any elephant horde or to come to think of it, any animal of any sort. There was a dilapidated building of a bygone era at the top and a solitary tea shack for mavericks like us. The tea seller was merely a teenaged boy and must have been a resident of some nearby village, which we had not noticed. We ordered some tea and more out of gratefulness and charity added some hard, almost inedible rusk biscuits to our orders. The effort, labour, and sweat that we had spent during the uphill trek was more than compensated by the cool breeze drying our sweat when we eventually reached the hill top. We could see the literally golden River Subaranarekha meandering in the distant, wide valley below, and the smoke blowing out of even more distant chimneys of unrecognizable factories and blast furnaces.

All four of us were city-bred, although we had been brought up in different cities and in different parts of the country. Gautam was quite a maverick and had participated in many amateur treks during his college days. He had carried on with his passion even after joining work, and was always on the lookout for a vacation, to tag along with an amateur hiking group on their treks to mountains and forests. More often than not we would realize about his adventures only after he had come back with a sun-tanned face, even darker than his usual. Rajiv and Alok were physically fit although not as adventurous as Gautam. Though not really a sportsman, I was nevertheless, fit enough to avoid embarrassment. So our group of four would often embark on some trek to nearby hills, forests, or waterfalls of the nearby Chota Nagpur area.

The tea shack on the top of the Dalma hill was run by a

barely teenaged boy called Arun, who lived in a nearby village and would trek to the top of the Dalma every fair weather day, to ply his trade in the distant hope that some so-called adventurous tourist or hiker would come up, and buy something from him. It must have been a hard and monotonous life, but he seemed to be happy and cheerful. Maybe, the lack of expectations from life and the ability to live from day to day was what separated that simple-minded Santhal boy of Chota Nagpur from us city-bred discontended youths of modern age. We, apparently, had everything going for us—we had no obvious deprivation to count, and yet were anxious of our future, dissatisfied with our present, wanting a better life although, though not very sure of which kind.

But on that weekend afternoon, sitting under the clear blue sky, on top of the green Dalma hill, with the invisible birds chirping, as our eyes and minds relaxed and our muscles tired, our uncertain future and mundane past appeared irrelevant. We realized that the most precious parts of our lives were such beautiful and yet simple moments, which come to us only rarely, separated from each other and from our 'other' lives—those that unfortunately define us,—and which we, even more unfortunately, identify with, in our follies.

By late afternoon, we were back at the foothill, soaked by a sudden, short afternoon shower, and headed to our restaurant-dhaba and bikes. We were four, famished youngsters by this time and also tired. We spent the next two hours, gorging on tandoori chicken, sipping cold lager beer, and enjoying the afternoon sun, slowly and lazily going down. We talked and talked of our past, present, and possible future, laughing, disputing, and lazing around till the inevitable time came for our journey back to Jamshedpur, our hostel rooms, duties of the next day— back to our 'other' lives.

17

Although Riya would return to India for her first vacation only after a year or so, I could avail of, if I so wanted, my vacations much before. I decided to take a seven-day break in the last week of December. Otherwise, my casual leaves would have lapsed and, although I was not really missing my home or parents, I felt I owed it to them and especially to my mother. Though they neither really needed it nor ever asked for it, I had saved my first salary for my mother— not out of emotions or convictions but just to make her happy. It was a sort of deliberate attempt to make it clear that she still exercised silent authority over her otherwise wayward son. It did make her happy. I also learnt that after I had left for Jamshedpur, my father had, unknown to me, thrown a party for his friends and relatives, few as there were, to celebrate my employment and the beginning of my earning days.

It was a bitterly cold and foggy Delhi that greeted me that December when I returned from Jamshedpur for my break. It had been a few years since I had spent any length of time in Delhi without Riya. I felt totally alone as most of my friends had also either moved out of Delhi or lived too far away from my south Delhi address. During that brief vacation in Delhi, finding myself at loose ends, I visited a number of familiar places where I and Riya used to spend hours together, chatting, laughing, and looking at each other, only a few months ago. But the hours seemed to be unbearably long and the bills of the restaurants unnecessarily high. I was sort of bored but was not really missing Riya as much as I had expected to.

Although, most of my friends and college mates had moved away, and got on with their lives, Rajesh was there. He was still living with his parents in his father's government quarters, and had got a job through campus recruitment, in a large, Indian, air conditioner manufacturing company. He was commuting every day for more than two hours in DTC buses to reach his factory-cum-office in the suburbs. So it was only on the solitary weekend during my brief vacation, that we could meet up over lunch, in our old, familiar south Indian restaurant, near our old college's gate. It was almost like old times, as we ordered dosas and exchanged notes about our respective lives. My world had changed more than Rajesh's with relocating to a different city, completely new environment, and a new set of friends. I was living on my own. Soon we realized that our worlds were no longer the same and it was difficult to find common grounds for conversation. Inevitably, we started talking about our old common college friends.

'So Ravi has gone back to Pune and has joined his father's business. I think he will stick to that. After all, he need not look for a job with a loaded father like his,' Rajesh explained about Ravi Gupta, one of our common friends.

'Piyush has got a job in Jamshedpur, in another TATA Company. He got his job through connections, I guess,' I said.

Rajesh was careful about not broaching the subject of Riya. I guess he feared that the topic might hurt me; although I am sure he was curious.

'Do you intend to continue with Red Star? The commuting must be taking a toll on you?' I enquired, feeling genuinely concerned and also thanking my stars that I was not in Rajesh's shoes.

'Let's see. I intend to go through the company's training programme, learn the tricks of the sales trade and then maybe change. But I am not looking to chuck this job immediately, either. The commuting is difficult, but I think I am learning. What about you?' Rajesh asked.

'I am quite comfortable, at least, as of now. I have only one concern that in such a large company I seem to get lost. Still, life is good,' I consoled myself.

'Vivek has joined Bharat Electronics through quota. I met him couple of weeks ago. He seems to be quite happy and content,' Rajesh said. Vivek was one of our former classmates, who had also shared the same University special bus.

We continued our pleasant, small conversation as we sat across the table, finishing our meals, looking through the full glass-paned walls to the busy streets below. Though it was a weekend, students from the two hostels of our college were wandering around in small groups, looking for a cheap meal or after-meal cigarettes. Although we had left our colleges only a few months back, we couldn't see a single familiar face, at least from the distance. After paying our bills, we travelled back together, for most of the way, to our homes, and increasingly separated lives.

My vacation passed, spending time in solitary

wanderings and in dutiful conversations at home. Soon it was time for me to head back to the north Delhi Railway station, one early and still darkish morning, to board the train for a thirty-six hours lonely journey to Jamshedpur. I almost felt like I was returning to my own home, although I had barely lived in Jamshedpur for a few months, and had virtually grown up in Delhi.

18

Mr Kulkarni was a devout, god-fearing gentleman, who had risen from the ranks and now in his fifties, he worked in my department as a manager, where I was eventually posted, after my six months of training. Although the formal training was over, we continued to be designated as graduate engineer trainees for almost two complete years. We—Mr Kulkarni and I—were both working at that time in a department where the principal job was to draw jigs and fixtures for different products to be machined. It was long, monotonous, and manual work and our drawing boards were placed adjacent to each other, overlooking the open rough grounds from the first floor windows that formed almost the entire eastern wall of the large hall that housed the department. Computer-aided drawing was still in its infancy and we were accustomed to drawing manually with drawing boards, drafting machines, pencils, and pens.

We would occasionally take breaks, in between our drawings. Although the work was difficult, we were hardly ever pressed for time and were not stressed unnecessarily. The company was doing well in the pre-liberalization errand when whatever could be produced by the factory was being gobbled up by consumers, who hardly had any choice. The consistent profits and sales figures resulted in a complacent and easy life for all in the company. The absence of cut-throat competition in the market meant every one of us, including our bosses could take it easy, and we could have our breaks.

'So Kulkarniji, what brought you to Jamshedpur from distant Maharashtra?' I asked him during tea break, one morning.

'Although I am proud of being a Maharashtrian as most Maharashtrians do, at least from the time of Shivaji, I was actually born and brought up here in Jamshedpur. My late father had migrated here for employment. We were service class people and didn't have land or anything. So we shifted,' Mr Kulkarni explained.

'And you never thought of going back to your hometown?' I enquired.

'No. Now this is my hometown. I was born and brought up here and so is my daughter. True, we have relatives in Maharashtra who sometimes visit or we visit them. But for all practical reasons, all the people whom I have known in my life, are from here. I would be a total stranger if I were to go back to my so-called hometown. But then, my case is not very unique in this company. If you look around yourself, even in this small department, or in your hostel, people from all across India have come to stay here, over generations, in search for decent employment, and have stayed back,' Mr Kulkarni said.

The company, I knew, preferred employing the kin of people who have already worked there. A policy, which seemed to have worked for the company and its employees, at least, up to that point in time.

People, who wanted decent employment, steady and secure lives, were quite satisfied to work for the company and live in its clean, but isolated township. But increasingly, it was finding it rather difficult to keep the ambitious and restless young men of my generation satisfied, who wanted more out of life. Satellite television had started beaming in our homes, MNCs had come to stay and offer lucrative salaries. Settling abroad was a real option, as Riya had found out, and many of my generation were feeling stifled in the secure but unadventurous life of working and living in the 75-year-old company.

The drawing board and table immediately in front of Mr Kulkarni's were always vacant and were deliberately kept so. When I asked one day, Mr Kulkarni explained, 'It belonged to Mr Murthy. He was from Andhra. He died in a railway accident while travelling to his home town on a vacation two years ago. He was young and had just married a couple of years back. We have kept his drawing board and space empty since then. It is difficult for any of us, who worked with him day after day, under the same roof, to use that board. I can almost see Murthy working on that board, chuckling to himself and talking to me.'

I was sure that sooner or later, Murthy's board and table would eventually be occupied by somebody, maybe after Mr Kulkarni's retirement. Nothing in life remains vacant for anybody forever. I wondered where and how Murthy's wife was but refrained from asking further, and went back to work.

So life went by in between my friends of Engineer's Hall, drawing jigs and fixtures in office, in occasional treks and eating out, reading, and writing letters to Riya, dutiful telephone calls from STD booths to home, friendly loneliness and mental solitude, and regular restlessness and steady dissatisfaction.

19

It was Ganesh Chaturthi and Mr Kulkarni had invited me to his home for a meal in the evening. Ganesh Chaturthi was not a sanctioned holiday by the company. In fact, we had very few holidays in the factory apart from the weekly Sunday, maybe half a dozen or so for the entire year. The factory was open even on Diwali, arguably the most popular festival—the festival of lights—celebrated all over northern India. Ganesh Chaturthi was not a local festival and only the Maharashtrians celebrated it, that too in their homes. There were no street processions or public immersions of the Ganesh idol in the city on the day.

I realized then that Mr Kulkarni had lost his wife years ago. Somehow I had been expecting a normal, happy family, with the lady of the house being a rolly-polly, aunt-like figure welcoming and feeding me and offering after-dinner sweets. It had never occurred to me that it could be otherwise. And so it was a shock to find Mr Kulkarni and his daughter Kajal as the only two figures in the house. They welcomed me with utmost sincerity without making too much of a show.

It was a rainy day and the drawing room was nice, clean and cheery, and had an uncluttered look about it where I settled down. But somehow the drawing room and its occupants gave the impression that the entire house was maintained in the same way and no special efforts were done to impress the guests. Both father and daughter seemed similar—simple down to earth, honest, and warm people, full of self-effacing humility and yet quietly confident, which made any showing off unnecessary.

Apparently, there were no servants in the house or even if there were, they were in the kitchen and invisible to me. Kajal served some fresh fruit juice to us and took a glass herself, and confidently joined us in our pre-dinner conversation. It was not possible for me to guess her age from her looks. She must have been about my age or maybe a couple of years older, but I could not tell for sure.

Out of politeness, I interrupted my conversation with Mr Kulkarni, who was about to embark on his postulation on the historical significance of Ganesh Chaturthi, to enquire about Kajal's studies.

'So, do you study?' I asked Kajal.

'No. I finished my PG a couple of years back,' She answered. So she was definitely older than me although it didn't show.

'She was a good student too! She had come first in her PG here. Both her professor and I wanted her to do PhD but she didn't,' Mr Kulkarni smiled.

'Why not?' I enquired, asking the question to no one in particular.

Kajal hesitated a bit before answering, 'I was not inclined to spend the energy and time that is really required to do thorough research. I was just not intellectually curious enough and I didn't want to do a PhD only because I was a good student.'

That was an exceptional answer from Kajal that showed that she had remarkably confident views, and was not afraid to stay on her own chosen course.

She had finished her studies then and I thought better not to ask her any further questions about her lest I should be considered unusually curious about her. Although, even with that short acquaintance then, I could not make myself believe that this remarkable woman would be spending her time merely waiting for marriage.

It was drizzling outside and the sound of raindrops falling on loose tin roofs nearby was drifting in through the open windows, setting the background to our conversation as we sat for our meal. Kajal served the food and joined us. It was the first time I had puran poli—a kind of sweet pancake—a typical Maharashtrian dish, I was to learn. But they had cared to prepare some fish fries too, maybe keeping in mind my Bengali origins. During conversation, Mr Kulkarni ventured to say that Kajal was working voluntarily for a local NGO called Gram Swarajya Samiti—the village self-government committee. What he meant was Kajal was not getting paid for her work with the NGO. I was curious as at that time NGOs had not become so fashionable, especially in the small towns in India.

'What sort of work does the NGO do?' I asked.

'It works in many fields among the tribal villages of this district—self-employment, education, health, etc. Sometimes I train their teachers and also work among the tribal women to ensure their self-reliance and economic empowerment. But there is no hard and fast rule as in offices. We all do all sort of things as the need arises,' Kajal explained without any hesitation this time. She seemed to talk quite frankly with me.

The homemade shreekhand was delicious—cold and very sweet. I had managed to over eat. This was the first time I had had the chance to eat a homemade meal since I had left home. I thanked Mr Kulkarni for it, although I should have thanked both the father and the daughter for the delightful evening. Somehow my innate shyness stopped me from thanking Kajal directly. The drizzle had stopped and amidst the sounds of croaking frogs, I bid them adieu to return to my hostel. I suddenly realized that it was almost midnight and that time had passed so quickly and effortlessly and that I was not tired at all despite the long working day.

20

Riya was supposed to visit India during the Christmas and New Year vacations of her University—which were still a couple of months away. Although we were regularly exchanging letters, it had been more than a year since we had sat face-to-face, or I had heard her voice. The ISD calls were considered unimaginably expensive in those days. Even our letters were becoming monotonous as we couldn't find things to write about that we thought the other could relate to. Our acquaintances, our friends, our surrounding environment, our work—all were so different. It was, for example, difficult for me to imagine her in snow-covered streets in sub-zero temperature, as she wrote, having never seen snowfall in my life. Nevertheless and maybe because of that, I was eagerly looking forward to Riya's first visit to India, and had already got my leave sanctioned and tickets booked to Delhi. My leave-sanctioning authority was only Mr Kulkarni as he was the singular manager of our department. He, however, had never made us realize that. Neither had the work ever seemed to suffer because of his apparent lack in exercising his legitimate authority. Though he never asked and I am sure would have never asked, I told him the reason behind my intended leave. It was my inherent tendency to show off the fact that I was smart enough to have a girlfriend. Although I was not engaged to Riya, I referred to her as my fiancée to Mr Kulkarni, in want of any other suitable name. To call her simply my girlfriend, I thought, didn't give full meaning to my serious intentions.

In those days, the graduate engineer trainees working for any of the TATA companies were considered 'prize catches' in the marriage market of Jamshedpur, to put it very crudely. The reality was that many of the senior executives and managers liked to get their daughters who had reached a certain age, married to suitable—in terms of caste, community, and economic conditions of the parents—graduate engineer trainees. It was the most natural desire for them and I could not find anything wrong in that, although there was a general derision in the way this phenomenon was alluded to, in egoistical boastings among my young and ambitious bachelor hostel mates.

Since that first delightful dinner, I visited Mr Kulkarni's house a few times and had developed easy social familiarity with both father and daughter. Some of my hostel mates had noticed my not-so-frequent visits and had already warned me against Mr Kulkarni's possible intentions to get me married to his daughter. I knew Mr Kulkarni far better, but still thought I should openly tell him about Riya and so I did. As expected, the manners and behaviour of Mr Kulkarni didn't show even an iota of change and he was as friendly and welcoming to me as before, much to my relief. Whether he shared his knowledge about Riya with Kajal, I didn't know. To me, at least at that time, it didn't seem important enough.

As I was about to complete my first year in the company,

my roommate moved out to his independent quarters in anticipation of his impending marriage. My new roommate was as different from the previous one, at least in his behaviour and manners, as chalk is to cheese. He was loud and foul-mouthed, but had a good heart. It was his cultural upbringing in the heartlands of north India which made him that way. Though he could be quite uncouth with others, because of some unfathomable reason, he always respected my privacy and never intruded into topics that I didn't care to share. Dinesh was in many ways a very enigmatic character, full of contradictions, and we shared a lovely relationship as roommates.

21

Although I had undertaken the thirty-six hours long train journey from Jamshedpur to Delhi on earlier occasions too, this time there was a sense of eager anticipation as I knew I would be meeting Riya after fifteen months. Also this time it was winter and although the night was cold in the second class carriage that I was travelling in, the waking hours were pleasant, and generally reflected my positive outlook on life, in that journey.

It was very early in the morning when the Muri Express departed from the Tatanagar Railway station. After a short nap as I woke up and gazed out through the open grilled windows of the railway carriage, the train had already left the industrial suburbs of Jamshedpur, and was trudging away contently through the heart of the Chota Nagpur plateau. It passed open, empty, red-soiled fields, interspersed with deep sal forests with splashes of shocking bright, red wild flowers here and there.

A long train journey through the length and breadth of India opens one's eyes to the diversity and sheer vastness of the country. The placid, sparsely populated, and peaceful rural surroundings of the Chota Nagpur plateau soon transformed into emerald green, freshly sown wheat fields as the train crossed into eastern Uttar Pradesh. One could now see densely populated villages, dusty, unplanned mofussil towns, rundown traffic, and chaos which this fertile soil supported and kind of encouraged. Even the railway stations were overcrowded, chaotic, dirty, and noisier than most I had seen, as if there was something simmering somewhere beneath the surface of calm, waiting to explode at the slightest of pretexts. The train travelled through the fertile Indo-Gangetic plains throughout the next day and the rural landscape remained pleasantly green and soothing till it reached the shabby, suburban areas surrounding Delhi, the next morning. The sheer and stark ugliness of the suburban surroundings caused by urbanization was a reminder of how man had no aesthetic sense as compared to his creator.

Riya was supposed to reach Delhi the same night as me. But once again I refrained myself from going to the airport to receive her. This tendency to restrain oneself, of not going all out to express one's feelings, was perhaps natural to my generation. The next day when we met, at a neutral ground, in one of our old meeting places, I found myself examining Riya critically, trying to find out whether, and in what manner, she had changed over the past fifteen months of our separation—whether and how the USA and her experiences had changed her, her thoughts, and especially, her feelings for me.

If there was one thing special about Riya, it was her complete spontaneity and confidence. If anything she was even more exuberant than her old self. Naturally, she was full of experiences of her University life in the USA—less of her studies but more about her overall experiences, her surroundings, her friends, her excursions, the sheer beautiful, comfortable, and hassle-free life of the USA. Her studies were also going well and I thought she had developed into a more interested and keen student than I had known her to be. At the same time she had retained her sense of fun as before. In fact, she seemed to be totally happy, satisfied, and absorbed with her life there and had no complaints. She still had at least nine months till she would finish her course for master's degree. I didn't dare broach the subject of her plans after her post-graduation and she didn't seem to be in any hurry.

It was a beautiful Delhi winter day—sunny and shiny, and at least that part of central Delhi where we were having our lunch, looked beautiful. There was a slight breeze and the dry leaves, having fallen from the ancient pre-New Delhi trees were swirling in it, dancing intricately on the paved footpaths.

'Although there are a couple of Indian restaurants in my University city, they are frightfully expensive and even there the food is a little bland for the Indian taste. This is the first time I am having kulfi since I left India,' Riya said, looking at the kulfi–faluda which was being served by the same old waiter who used to serve us earlier in our college days.

'Did you miss Indian food?' I queried.

'Indian food, movies, and cricket are the only three things that I really missed in the USA,' Riya replied. 'And of course, you, mom, dad and my brother,' she added, almost as an afterthought.

Compared to Riya's experiences in the USA, I had nothing much to say about my life in Jamshedpur and she didn't seem too eager to know about them, anyway. It appeared to me that she was deliberately avoiding any talk of the future or about my different life in India. She was passionately happy about her life in the USA, and of the overall experience, and made no bones about it. Somehow, my entire growing up had induced in me the thought that such full-throated bodily enjoyment of life was laced with guilt and uncertainty; as if such happiness and joy were fragile, unreal, and somehow at the cost of others. My laughter was never as open and full as those of Riya's and her friends.

22

For most of the days of the fortnight-long vacation, Riya and I went to our old and familiar meeting points although now because I was earning, we could afford to go to more expensive joints. Sometimes, some of Riya's old friends, who continued to live in Delhi, having mostly joined their family businesses, joined us. They were also eager to meet Riya after such a long break, popular as she always was with them. Most of them knew me too from college days, and although I was quite clearly not one of 'them,' they indulged me in a light-hearted and friendly way.

The days were short as they always are in winter but during that fortnight in Delhi, the days appeared to be shorter and flew faster than one could have imagined. Soon it was time for Riya to fly back to her University, leaving her once familiar life and me, again.

Back in Jamshedpur, my life, I realized, was clearly divided into two distinct parts, cleanly sliced by distance. My life, factory, friends, and colleagues in Jamshedpur had nothing in common with my life, parents, Riya, and old acquaintances of Delhi. Switching between the two made me feel like a person living a dual life. I had no idea where and how the two distinct worlds would ever reach a meeting point. Sometimes I wondered whether I would have to choose one of the two. Although I loved and missed Riya, living in Jamshedpur, with my newly-acquired financial and other independences, gave me freedom to lead a life, unburdened by past. I loved that life too, which was my own, for the first time in my life. This was also the first time that I was living completely on my own terms, and although I was away from my loved ones, the sense of freedom and confidence that this life had induced in me was like the arrival of manhood in a young boy. I really didn't know what to do with my future as it appeared to be beholden to Riya, whose plans appeared to be yet hazy and uncertain, somewhere across the Atlantic Ocean. The ability or the good fortune to be able to live in the present is something very few of us are blessed with. The wish to embrace the possible concerns about the future, losing track of happiness in the present, is something which is more common and one that can be imagined.

Although I was quite close to my new roommate and I had other friends, who were fellow graduate engineer trainees mostly, and with whom I shared the hostel, I could never bring myself to talk openly about my uncertainties with them, especially when they bordered on Riya. On many nights over the weekends, we would sit on the bare floors of one of the long mosaic corridors of the hostel, a group of four or five, drinking and smoking late into the night, talking to each other, but mainly to ourselves. The others present mostly would become receptive sound boxes, while we unburdened ourselves of our past, thoughts about possible future, concerns, views of the world, factory, politics, books, and philosophies. We would argue passionately about the merits and demerits of the

Ramjanmabhoomi movement, about India's prospects at the world cup (cricket, of course), and about how we would surely stagnate if we continue to work in the same company. But quite remarkably, none of us ever discussed our girlfriends or other girls even remotely, delegating such personal issues in a zone which was not to be shared.

This was also the time when, perhaps because of the effect of other hostel mates, worldly ambitious as some of them undoubtedly were, I started rethinking about what I would like to do with my future. My uncertainties with Riya and her life in the USA were being doubly compounded by my own doubts about what I wanted to do with my own life and future.

I was earning a decent salary and was comfortably placed in a secure job, which held fair prospects of growth. But when you are twenty years old, it is difficult to feel satisfied with whatever life brings to you. Having been brought up in a particular culture, the prospect of making money for money's sake didn't attract me as a worthy pursuit in life. Not that I didn't recognize the worth of money, but to me it was merely a means to have a decent and relatively comfortable life, to take care of one's worldly requirements and responsibilities. I felt the need to discover a higher purpose in life, to explore whether there indeed exists anything like 'one's calling'. My job as a graduate engineer trainee somehow didn't fulfill my need of a purpose. I sometimes felt like a member of a gang of automatons, working from seven to four everyday, to earn my monthly salary. Of course, such questions and periods of self doubts were rare. I was mostly occupied and absorbed with my day to day activities—waking up, getting ready, rushing to office so as not to be marked late, working on my drawing board, talking to colleagues, going out to dinner, hanging out with hostel mates, taking occasional weekend treks and reading esoteric books of Richard Bach and Paulo Coelho. Still, rare as they were, they continued to exist.

23

'Are you happy?' I asked Kajal, sitting across her at the dining table in their home. Her father was not at home and I had reached a stage of easy familiarity with the family where I could easily spend time with Kajal in her father's absence without any awkwardness or formality. Also, you don't ask everyone such stupid questions.

Remarkably, Kajal didn't find the question stupid. It merited her attention and silence, and moreover it is never easy to answer such questions. They never have absolute answers, for most of us, at most times.

'I guess, yes. Of course, there are times when I do feel low, especially when my mind wanders to the past.'

It was as if Kajal had some past experiences, memories of which made her occasionally sad. Thinking of sorrowful experiences of the past often makes us unhappy, but thinking of happy incidents of the past that have no chance of recurring, sometimes makes us feel even worse. Only a child is capable of completely living in the present.

'Why?' I didn't know whether I should have asked.

'Maybe you don't know yet but I was married to Murthy exactly a month before he met with the fatal train accident,' Kajal said. She was looking out of the window at nothing in particular, with a sort of long-sighted look, as if trying to avoid eye contact.

I was shocked as I had never imagined that Kajal had gone through such a painful and recent trauma in her life. She had always seemed to be in control with no trace of self-pity or sadness in her behaviour. Even Mr Kulkarni had never given away anything—working with me, day in and day out, in the same hall, within a short distance of the empty drawing board, where his son-in-law used to work, not so long ago—the one, who had been married to his only daughter, barely a month before he was taken away permanently and cruelly by the uncertain claws of destiny.

It was turning dark outside. The sound of the intermittent traffic from the road floated in through the open windows. Noticing that I was too shocked to react, Kajal herself continued. 'But life goes on and the initial shock melts away. The important thing is not to fall into the trap of self-pity. Of course, I had my father who has been a real support all through,' she said.

I still didn't know what to say. I kept playing and tinkering with the cup that Kajal had served tea in, sometime back. I had never known a person who had suffered such an untimely tragedy in her life. We take so many things in our lives for granted, I realized.

'Would you like to see sometime what kind of work we do in the villages?' Kajal asked, maybe to inject some words into the silence that was turning awkward.

'Yes. Why not? It will be a change from the routine of factory–hostel life. I can come along on any of the weekly offs from the factory,' I replied.

'That's fine. So let's go this Sunday. I don't like to postpone things any longer. We will take the seven thirty bus from the bus stand opposite our house, if it is okay with you,' Kajal said. 'This might be your first visit to a tribal village.'

'That's fine with me,' I replied, thinking that it would be the very first time that I would be visiting any village, let alone a tribal one. In our family, the last one to have had any connections with life in the village was my great-grandfather. He had worked as the 'naib' or assistant to a wealthy zamindar or landlord of eastern Bengal. Since my grandfather's days, we had always been city-bred with no remnants of any umbilical cord tying us to our forefathers' village, and whatever chances there might have existed to re-establish any such contact, had simply vanished into thin air with the partition.

I was about to leave, when Mr Kulkarni entered the house and having heard of our recently concluded plans, heartily endorsed them.

'I have not seen what kind of work Kajal and her organization is doing, but I am sure that if Kajal is involved, it must be worthwhile. If nothing else, you will get to see the beauty of the countryside. The weather is wonderful at this time of the year,' Mr Kulkarni said. It was early February and the weather was indeed blissful.

'Why don't you join us?' I suggested, more out of politeness than anything else. I realized that something inside me desperately wanted him to refuse.

'You forget that our weekly offs are on different days of the week,' Mr Kulkarni replied, smiling. Despite my protests, the sincere exhortations of the father daughter duo once again compelled me, not altogether against my inner wishes, to have dinner that evening too at their home, before returning to my hostel room.

24

I walked from my hostel, on that cool Sunday spring morning, to the bus stop. There was some unknown tree, in wild blossom, bending over the stop, which was marked just by a solitary metal pole at the side of the street, with an attached signage.

Kajal joined me barely two minutes later. She was wearing a crisp, light, cream-coloured cotton sari and had obviously taken a bath in the morning as her hair was still damp. The bus was late but it was very pleasant, and since I was not in any hurry, I didn't mind waiting at all. There was a slight cool breeze and the morning light had that quality which one gets to see very rarely. It seemed that it had rained somewhere nearby overnight.

'Hello. Have you been waiting for long?' Kajal asked.

'No, only for a few minutes or so. But it is rather nice, the freshness and coolness of this morning,' I replied.

'Yes. The bus might be late though. It usually is, but it does arrive eventually,' Kajal smiled.

Presently, the ramshackle minibus, painted chocolate and chrome, arrived with a thick, grayish cloud trailing behind it. It was a private operator-run bus, an old and long extinct model of TELCO that my present employer would like to forget about. The driver, a rakish, tribal, young man, bare chested and wearing a garish red bandana, brought the bus to a halt but didn't dare switch off the engine. We were the only passengers to board the full but not overcrowded bus.

Kajal managed to get a window seat and after only about five minutes or so, as her fellow passenger—a grey stubbled, bespectacled oldish gentleman disembarked—I occupied the aisle seat beside her. The bus had left the city and after crossing the bridge over the river, it had moved directly into the tribal hinterland, leaving the TATA island behind, both literally and metaphorically.

'You know, I used to think you are a big snob,' Kajal said suddenly, craning her neck to look at me.

'Actually, it is nothing very extraordinary. It is quite a common opinion among people. But it is nevertheless a mistaken notion. It is probably my innate introvert and shyness that makes me a little wary of opening up to people whom I don't know too well. That is taken as a sign of arrogance. It has happened to me many times, in my college days too. I guess, even in my hostel, many of my colleagues believe I am arrogant and a snob. Can't help it,' I replied.

'You don't really care, do you? And that too is quite apparent,' Kajal smiled. I smiled back, looking at the scenery beyond the open window, averting Kajal's eyes.

The bus was meandering through reddish brown, empty fields with a green patch here and there. Sometimes I could see a tribal village, sparsely populated, with reddish, ochre-coloured mud walled houses with paintings of white chalk on them, with neatly swept open courtyards, and old wizened tribal women weaving baskets of bamboo.

After only about an hour of driving on these roads, which were increasingly becoming bumpy, we arrived at our destination—a village—at least for that journey, on our first day trip together.

25

The village was called Laldih, Kajal informed as we got down from the bus. The origin of the numerous names of the numerous villages and towns, with some names sometimes repeating, separated by hundreds and thousands of miles, have always intrigued me. There is bound to be a story, a reason behind each of the names, most of the time hidden behind the veil of centuries unknown. Kajal's NGO, had been working in Laldih for a few years and it was one of the first villages in the entire region where the organization had started its work of women's self-employment, education, and health activities.

We walked on the unpaved, dusty lanes of the village, past a greenish pond on our right, amidst rows of mud-walled tribal houses, till we reached a place from where we could hear children shouting afar. It was an open school, in every sense of the word, where a young woman was trying to maintain a semblance of teaching amidst some forty odd students of various age groups and heights, assembled in an open mud yard, in front of a rough, greyish black wooden board.

As we approached the school, the dark-skinned, young teacher gave Kajal an open and affectionate smile, and her face lit up in genuine joy and apparent relief. Most of the children also seemed to recognize Kajal, but were more curious than thrilled.

Kajal introduced me. She said, 'This is Pankaj saheb.' Why she added the colonial sounding 'saheb' suffix to my good enough name, I had no idea. 'I asked him to come with me and look at what work we are doing,' she added as a way of explanation.

The young teacher, whom Kajal introduced as Vandana, simply and generously smiled. Her class had been interrupted and some of the kids were getting restless.

'Are the studies going well? Is there any problem in teaching?' Kajal asked Vandana.

'No didi,' Vandana said, smiling again, revealing once more her shiny white teeth, which looked brighter against her dark, smooth, and oily skin.

With my usual city-bred cynicism, I was not sure what good the school, with its blatantly inadequate infrastructure and facilities, taught by an apparently half educated and clearly untrained teacher, was doing to the hapless children, who were definitely first generation learners with no educational support at all in their homes. I moved around the kids and tried to evaluate, by cursorily looking at their slates and at a rare notebook, their level of studies and learning. It was difficult to tell as the kids were of different ages and I didn't know what they had been taught. It was all haphazard and chaotic but the teaching didn't lack earnestness and sincerity. It was apparent that both Kajal and Vandana more so, loved the children and liked teaching them. This overflowing love somehow attempted to overcome the limitations imposed by lack of facilities, and cold professionalism.

By this time, Kajal was inquiring about the children who were absent on that day. I was surprised to see that there were only two children in the entire village, who had not appeared that Sunday and that too because of sickness. Kajal satisfied herself by looking at some of the children's notebooks randomly, and at a sort of teacher's diary of Vandana's. It seemed that the studies were up to her expectations. She then bid farewell to the teachers and students, who replied with a full-throated 'Namaste didi.'

The sun was already up and it was getting hot although it was only early spring. We walked on the dusty lanes of the village to a sort of open space in front of a neat brick and mortar building, probably the only one in this village of mud houses. A small, painted board proclaimed the name of the organization for which Kajal worked on a voluntary basis: 'Gram Swarjya Samiti', GSS for short— meaning village self-government organization in Hindi— although for the local tribals, Hindi of the Indo-Gangatic plain was almost as foreign as the distant English. I could not tell whether this was the headquarters of the NGO or merely one of its centres. There was a small garden-like space immediately in front of the building. The flowers and green bushes were carefully watered and maintained, appearing a little foreign, and out of place but at the same time, were welcoming to the eyes, among the reddish dusty surroundings. The building itself was very much 'a work in progress' with reddish-brown steel girders raising their collective heads over the roof and new, bare, brick facades showing at the sides.

There was a small office type of a room at one end of the rectangular verandah which stretched in front of the building. The verandah itself was neat and empty, but in the large hall attached to the verandah and immediately next to it, many women were sitting on the floor and were engaged in manual work with great industry. As Kajal led me into the hall, after having deposited our footwears outside and having rinsed our dusty feet and hands with the water from the hand pump situated next to the garden, many curious eyes looked up together at me.

Around a dozen tribal women, wearing immaculately clean sarees, and plastic gloves were engaged in seasoning raw unripe mango pieces in spices and oil, as preparation for preserving them as pickles. The other women were engaged in the varied processes, involved in the production of papad. These were the self-employment initiatives of the society, Kajal explained to me. The society organized the women into groups, trained them, and provided the loan to buy the raw materials for the first time, guided and persevered with the women to make them regular and industrious and finally helped them market their produce. The women had managed to repay the initial loan and were saving decently for themselves. But more importantly they all seemed to be happily engaged in an activity that they owned and felt a sense of responsibility towards. Many of their children were studying in the nearby open-air school, run by the society itself. In short, Kajal and her NGO were slowly helping the women transform their lives and of their families. I wondered whether the experience of working in these sun-baked villages amongst these affectionate tribal women had transformed Kajal too in some way.

26

On that very first trip with Kajal to Laldih, I had been a tourist, more than anything else, trying to glimpse at Kajal and the organization's work at the so-called grassroot level. But even that first cursory glance at her work opened my urban, city-bred eyes to many new hitherto unknown revelations. For one, I got an insight into how very vast our country actually is and how many villages we have. I also came to realize the vast differences of space and centuries that separate these villages from the capital of India, from her so-called corridors of power, from the editorial rooms of our mainstream media, and from the collective minds of the English speaking, urban Indians like us—like that of Riya and me.

But in my subsequent visits with Kajal to Laldih and to other nearby villages, I was also touched by the collective affection and expectations of these simple, tribal villagers. I found that I actually enjoyed teaching and learning from the tribal children under the open sun much more than I had enjoyed giving tuitions in my youth to the children of the rich parents in Delhi. These children loved learning from me rather than from Vandana, and even she joined her students when I taught mathematics and science to the slightly grown up ones among them.

In one of these visits, Kajal took me to another nearby village called Neeldih to introduce me to the founder and the most important person of the GSS—a remarkable lady who was addressed by everybody, including Kajal, as Nirmaladi. Nirmaladi, with her salt-and-pepper hair and bespectacled eyes, must have been close to fifty when I met her for the first time. She was quite simply the noblest and sweetest human being that I had met till then or since. She was highly educated, as Kajal told me, and had worked as a professor in a university in the USA once, but had founded her NGO—GSS—and built it from virtually scratch, transforming the lives of so many families in the process. There must have been a remarkable story in her transformation, from a USA based professor to her present being, and there would be a strong reason behind that. But somehow she always made light of her past and concentrated on the future of the NGO. But despite her remarkable sacrifices and achievements, Nirmaladi was most affectionate to one and all and had a sweet smile and demeanour that made her everybody's favourite, including mine.

Kajal and the others had told her about me, but I didn't know the content of this exactly. As Kajal and I entered her office—a small but remarkably clean and organized room, with white-washed walls, she got up from her straight-backed wooden chair and welcomed me with a genuinely warm smile.

'Welcome to our small villages. Although I know that this is not your first trip, and I am so glad that you have returned after your first trip,' she said. This was Nirmaladi's first sentence to me. I uttered something incoherently and needlessly, praising her remarkable efforts, which she quickly brushed aside and got up to make some tea for all of us.

'I have heard that you have become quite popular among the villagers and especially among the kids, who really look forward to your visits and that is not only because of the sweets and toffees that you seem to carry for them from the city,' Nirmaladi remarked with her usual smile.

'That's nothing. I wish I could be of some use to the work that you all are doing here,' I said.

'Oh, there is plenty for all of us to do. The dearth of work is never a problem here or anywhere else for that matter,' Nirmaladi said in her immaculate English.

Kajal intervened in the conversation for the first time. 'I was thinking that if Pankaj is really interested, he can help us make contacts for selling our products in the city or even in Calcutta.'

'Yes, I can try and nowadays with internet and e-mail, making contacts and sending mails, etc., is quite easy,' I said, although I had absolutely no idea or experience about marketing anything but I didn't want to let Kajal down. It was the first time I had felt a sense of responsibility towards her, I realized later in our return journey to the city.

27

The brief spring had come and gone and the gulmohurs, planted neatly in rows on either side of central broad avenue of the township were in full bloom. Their orange-red flowers had hidden the leaves, and they really looked shockingly beautiful, especially against the stark, cloudless blue sky in the afternoon heat.

Riya had told me in her last letter that after that year-end exams that she had been busy preparing for, she had decided to use her vacation to take a trip across the USA with a few of her college friends. They would travel by road to the west coast to LA, Las Vegas and other places. She was excited and looking forward to it.

As before, her letters were remarkably regular, but I was beginning to realize that they had lost their previous spontaneity and were more an effort of labour rather than that of love. I could not blame her. Our worlds were getting more and more different and distant from each other, and the areas of convergence and commonality were reducing every month. Letters, however regular and well written they maybe, I realized are poor substitutes for conversations and in those days, international calls were totally unimaginable. Even STD calls to my family required me to trudge to some post office or more often to some privately owned STD booth, where one used to enter a tiny glass cubicle with ever-changing red LED figures showing the amount that one had to pay as one made polite greetings to one's parents or sister.

It was after one such phone call on a winter evening when I entered the Engineer's Hall—our hostel, that I distinctly felt an edge of excitement in the air. The atmosphere was a bit uncomfortable and uncertain. While I was still trying to figure out the reason for this sudden change in the hostel's environment, Khalid, our colleague and friend from Patna burst out, 'They finally destroyed it!'

He was angry, aghast, and inconsolable at the same time. I soon realized that the Babri Masjid at Ayodhya, the topic of intense speculation, controversy, anger, and opportunistic politics over the past few years, had been brought down by hordes of uncontrollable and violent people that day in Ayodhya, a religious and otherwise sleepy town in the northern Indian state of Uttar Pradesh. Many Hindus believed, or were led to believe, that the place where the Babri Masjid was built by the first Mughal Emperor of India, Babar—after whom the mosque was named—was where the ancient mythological-cum-historical, and religious Shri Ram Chandra was born. Although it had been recorded in historical papers that some local controversy had existed between the Hindus and Muslims of Ayodhya, over reclaiming the site for Hindu worship even in the time of British rule, it was only in our youth that we heard about the controversy for the first time when some political organizations decided to start a movement to reclaim the site of the Babri Masjid and build a temple dedicated to Ram. Eventually, the movement had grown, over the course of a few dramatic years and had spun out of control leading to the events of that day in December.

Khalid's sudden outburst was met with stony silence from others, who sat around the metal surfaced dining table, sipping their evening tea from glass tumblers. Not many—all Hindus—shared his deep sense of hurt, but thought it prudent to not react, at least at that very moment. Khalid looked around expectantly for support which was non-existent to his dismay. He grew defiant at this apparent lack of sympathy to his sense of hurt, and repeated this time less from the heart but more volubly, 'The bastards have actually pulled our mosque down. I knew beforehand that they would do so but nobody did anything. It's a shame. This country is no longer fit to live in.'

This time a couple of chaps, including my Hindu roommate from Aligarh glared back at Khalid challengingly, holding his stare and opposition. The situation had the potential to turn positively ugly, but someone decided to break up the conversation. Niloy said, 'It has been a long and tiring day. See you at dinner then.' As he rose, the rest of us got an opportunity to leave the dining room, which was turning acidic. Khalid remained our colleague and friend but after that evening of December, he never broached the subject of demolition of the Babri Masjid with any of us, ever.

28

During my holidays and in my free time, I had started getting involved with the affairs of GSS and although I didn't have the zeal of public service like that of Nirmaladi, I did feel more satisfied out of the work of GSS than of my salaried job—where I was drawing rather than designing jigs and fixtures.

The sound of the bells from some distant invisible temples was wafting in through the open wire-meshed window into the room, along with the cool breeze. We were in Neeldih, in our make shift dormitory where we—Nirmaladi, Kajal, and I—had decided to sleep. Kajal and I had missed the last bus going back to the city. I was naturally thinking about how worried Mr Kulkarni would be, in not finding Kajal at home that night. But Kajal and Nirmaladi appeared quite relaxed and calm as if it was common occurrence. It was still early in the evening and the darkness had engulfed the village only a few minutes back. There was a lantern in a corner of the room and its flickering flame was casting dancing shadows on the white-washed bare walls. We were sitting on our respective 'charpoys'—cots made of bamboo frame over which coconut fiber strings had been strung together. We had had an early evening meal of simple chapattis and daal and yet it was not late enough for any of us to go to sleep. I realized that in villages, evenings fell early and nights appeared to be far longer than in the cities with their numerous distractions of the modern electronic age.

Nirmaladi slowly took out her spectacles and carefully put them in their case. For the first time I could see her bare eyes that evening, in the light of the lantern. She looked younger without her specs but curiously enough her eyes looked tired at the same time.

Both out of a sense of long-suppressed curiosity and also to break the silence, I ventured to ask, 'Nirmaladi, what brought you to these villages in the first place? I mean, I understand that you were living somewhere else, a very different kind of life.' Kajal also looked up to Nirmaladi, expectantly, from her own cot, as if there were parts of Nirmaladi's story that even she did not know much about.

Nirmaladi looked at us, from one to another, and replied, 'It is a long story and it has been a long time too, but if you really want to know then there is no harm telling you two. Actually, I was not alone when I came here for the first time. Maybe, without John I would not, or rather could not, have ventured to my own homeland on my own. Kajal may have told you that I was teaching in the Harvard University in the USA. John was teaching there too, although our subjects and departments were different. He was a hydraulic–mechanical engineer.'

Nirmaladi paused to pour herself a glass of water from the earthen pot kept in the corner of the room. It was a starkly bare but fully functional room with everything essential in place but nothing superfluous. I thought I liked the bare functionality of the room, its cleanliness, its orderliness, its unpretentiousness, and its self-assuredness. In many ways, the room was a reflection of its occupant, as most living rooms are.

'And before you two young people jump to any conclusion, let me make it clear that we—John and I— were not linked romantically ever,' Nirmaladi continued. 'He was a very respected colleague and friend however. In his field of work, he invented a kind of handpump that could work on plateaus and hillocks, to get stored ground water up to the surface. He had thought that he could experiment and improve upon his invention here, by putting it to use in field situations, and at the same time help these villagers in solving one of their most basic of needs—that of safe drinking water. We discussed the possibilities. We had known each other and he knew that I was from India. At that time, I was young and was feeling a bit cramped and frustrated in the rarefied environs of academia. I wanted to do something in the so-called 'real world'. So one thing led to another and on one annual term end, we decided to take a long sabbatical and to come, and try our work in these villages of Chota Nagpur plateau. Of course, I didn't know then that I would stay on and that my life was taking an irreversible turn, as it eventually turned out to be,' Nirmaladi paused.

'When was all this?' I enquired, feeling that Nirmaladi's story had not ended. Kajal was silent but was an active listener. I wondered whether she was looking for some answers for her own life from Nirmaladi's story.

'Nineteen years ago. We decided to come to this part of India because of John, mainly. I myself had no prior experience of these places. Apart from the fact that the topography here supported John's experiments with his hand pump, he also had some connections with a Christian church working here—he was a devout protestant himself. That helped us to settle down in the initial years,' Nirmaladi continued. 'Although I am not a Christian myself, I do visit the church occasionally, and like their humanitarian work, especially, in the field of education,' she said.

'So where is John now?' I asked.

'John lived here for almost five years. He refined and perfected his invention and you can see his numerous handpumps working in these villages and beyond. They have been a boon to the lives and health of these villagers here, in a way, that is unimaginable for city-bred people like us,' Nirmaladi replied. 'True to his self, John never believed in, and never applied for any patent for his invention. Instead, he trained many local mechanics and artisans to make these handpumps and their parts based, on his design. His contribution is immense,' Nirmaladi paused. 'By the end of fifth year, his University finally refused to give him any further extension on his unpaid sabbatical and he was forced to make a decision to return to his world. By that time, his invention had become perfect and widespread, and he sort of felt that his purpose had been fulfilled. So he is back in the USA, teaching students Mechanical Engineering.'

'You didn't go back?' This time Kajal asked.

'No, I didn't. I also faced the same choice as John. The University refused to give us any further extension. So either I had to go back or quit my job, my security, and my world. And then I had to ask myself—which of the two worlds was mine and I decided that I should stay back. I quit my university job, and since then I have been here, living and working as you have seen,' Nirmaladi answered. 'By that time, these villagers had also become quite fond of me and in a way dependent on me, in a way in which my students in the University would never be.'

'Any regrets about your decision?' I ventured to ask.

'None, whatsoever. I am at peace with myself and my surroundings, and whenever I get to see young, modern, and educated people like you two, it is an additional bonus,' Nirmaladi smiled.

It was getting late in the night. Somewhere, in the village not very far, a dog was barking, and the silence amplified it. I could see through the open windows a solitary glow worm zig zagging across the opaque darkness in the verandah outside. Our conversation had reached an inevitable and slow end. Nirmaladi put the flame of the lantern at a minimum, taking care that the flame would not extinguish altogether and decided to retire, bidding both of us good night.

Before falling into a near dreamless sleep, I realized that it was the very first time in my life that I was sleeping in a village and that somehow I felt peaceful and relaxed. It was also the first time that I didn't think of Riya before falling asleep.

29

My work in office had increased, if not improved, at least in comparison to earlier months. The company had decided to enter into a joint venture with a USA company to produce diesel engines. Indian economy was opening up and such foreign collaborations were happening. We were in the process of designing the jigs and fixtures that would eventually be used in the machine shops of the factory of this new joint-venture company.

The work was heavy but extremely monotonous and frequently I found, especially on heavy, dull afternoons, that my mind was wandering while my hands were faithfully working on the drawing board. Right in front of our two-storeyed office building, visible through the glass windows, were the green, wild fields where the new factory was to soon come up. I could see Mr Kulkarni's back from my place, working away sincerely on his own drawing board, whereas he could easily, at his seniority, refrain from drawing, in the guise of 'supervising' others. But Mr Kulkarni was a different sort of man and his daughter a different sort of woman, as I had started noticing.

My interest and my visits to the work being done by GSS had become the cause that kept me and Kajal together, at least to start with. My day time office work, from nine in the morning to five in the evening, everyday, six days a week, provided me with my salary, which in its turn, gave me means of livelihood and a secure standing in an otherwise financially insecure society. But the source of my motivation and interest in life was now shifting towards whatever voluntary and honorary work I was able to do for Nirmaladi and Kajal's organization. Apart from the fact that I really thought that GSS's work was indeed useful, especially to the lives of those hundreds of villagers whom it touched, and also that I respected Nirmaladi's work and her sacrifice, it was my fear of disappointing Kajal that kept me working for them—especially when my salaried job's work load increased.

I had been able to manage a few long term contracts for GSS to supply kitchen condiments and pickles to the officer's mess of a few companies through my friends and colleagues. It was a very small effort but it helped many women in having steady source of cash, which enabled them to make some profit. The delight on their faces and the genuine appreciation from Nirmaladi and Kajal gladdened my heart much more than the increasing balance in my bank account ever did. In fact, I hardly deserved the amount of appreciation and praise that I got from the simple-minded village women, many of whom I had got to know by name. Many of them had started calling me 'Pankajda'—a kind of respectful address which literally would mean 'elder brother'. It was the first time anybody had addressed me thus.

'You don't talk so much about Riya nowadays,' Kajal said as a statement of fact. She was pouring tea from her kettle to awaiting cups, one for each one of us. We were sitting in the drawing room of her home.

'Is it? Why, I am going to meet her this Christmas. Riya will come to India in her Christmas–New Year break, and despite the increasing work load, I have managed to get seven days casual leave sanctioned at that time,' I replied, almost explaining myself.

'Yes. My father can't refuse you, or for that matter anybody else. But for once I wish he had not been so kind,' Kajal said almost without thought. It was as if the last sentence had slipped off her mind in a moment of unusual and unconscious carelessness. She laughed trying to make it appear like a joke, but it had not been said lightly.

I felt nice, appreciated, awkward, and confused at the same time, and a plethora of thoughts and feelings flooded into my being in an undecipherable manner. I just didn't know what to say although I wanted desperately to say something, anything to lighten Kajal's apparent awkwardness. I kept quiet.

30

Delhi was being whiplashed by torrents of unseasonal rain on the day my train arrived. The day was dark, cloudy, moist, and shiveringly cold. The evening was colder when Riya and I met. We were sitting in a pre-independence era restaurant in Connaught Place. I had ordered tea for myself and Riya had asked for a cup of cappuccino for herself. It was around that time that I had started to notice for the first time that there are many varieties in which coffee can be served and that what we believed to be espresso coffee— milk coffee through which steam had been passed—was not what the world termed as espresso.

Riya had arrived in India two days ago and was to leave for the USA after around two weeks.

'You could have at least taken two weeks' leave from your job.' It was the first thing that Riya said that evening. 'I have come all the way from the USA.'

I don't know whether she felt bad about me not being there during her holidays or for the fact that I had decided to leave Delhi before her return.

'I could not ask for any more leave at this juncture. The work load right now is quite high, and actually it was awfully kind of them to have sanctioned even this seven days casual leave,' I replied.

'Why, it is your due, isn't it?' Riya queried.

'Leave is never a matter of right. It always depends on the circumstances and work load. At least, this is how it goes here, in India.' I replied. 'Why don't you come along to Jamshedpur with me for one week and see how I live and work. After all, you might be living there as well after you finish your studies,' I added.

There was a deathly silence. I had broached a subject—the subject of our future—that we had been trying to avoid for the past few months. I had even started doubting whether there was any common future for us. Whether Riya's life—dreams, ambitions and ideas—could ever converge with my predictable pattern of visible future. But I didn't want to face my doubts.

'But you are living in a male bachelor's hostel, aren't you? Where will I go and stay? This is not the USA where I could easily park myself in your room,' Riya laughed, avoiding the larger question.

I could have said that she would be more than welcome to stay at Mr Kulkarni and Kajal's home but something stopped me. The idea of Riya staying in Jamshedpur, even for a short period, suddenly appeared to me to be totally incongruous, illogical, and even fantastical.

'So, what's up? How is your job going?' Riya asked me. 'You don't write too much nowadays.'

'It is heavy and boring,' I didn't specify whether I was talking about my job or my life. I tried to explain briefly about what I did for my living and how my company had entered into a joint venture with a USA company.

'Can't you get transferred to this joint venture? That way, maybe you can manage a posting in the USA?' Riya asked, suddenly interested.

I had never thought on those lines. Anyway the joint venture had been formed to manufacture engines in India, so the idea of Indian engineers going to the USA to work didn't seem too likely. Maybe, for a short training or so. I told Riya as much.

'But I know, you would not even try. You expect everything to be placed in your lap. The world does not work like that,' Riya's comment was sharp and quick.

I could have said much in my reply. I could have said that pushing one's own self to get a better life abroad was not my thing. I could have said that living in the USA was not everybody's dream. I could have told Riya about Nirmaladi who had seen and lived in the USA for far longer than Riya, and had quit that life for good to live and work in some of the most deprived of Indian villages. But I didn't say anything. I simply said. 'Yes. I know I am lazy and ambitionless.'

'And you make almost a virtue out of it. I don't understand.' But Riya really didn't want to understand.

My tea and Riya's cappuccino had long finished. The drizzle outside had come to a stop. The evening lights of Connaught Place were glittering through the water droplets suspended on the window panes. We were sitting across only a table but somehow the conversation appeared to be taking place across a vast distance—like across the Atlantic Ocean itself, and the voices were getting lost somewhere in between.

31

I met Riya's father on Christmas evening. Mr Malhotra had always been a proud man, and like all proud men, felt entitled to his pride. But now he had also become proud of Riya's education and how she was studying in the USA. We were all sitting in their drawing room. A new carpet, Persian I was told, adorned the floor.

'It is great pity that our politicians are destroying our universities. In my days one could study in an Indian university and still do well in life. But now they are like pits,' Mr Malhotra said.

I didn't comment. No comments were expected. Anyway, I had nothing to compare my experiences of Indian universities with. I had never been to a foreign university. I wondered if Mr Malhotra had. But he was right to some extent and one could see politicization of student unions leading to deterioration of the campus life. Unruly ruffians, in order to get a foothold in a political dream, were hobnobbing with political parties to capture student politics across the country. Not that the political parties were unwilling.

'So, what do you want to do with your future?' Mr Malhotra asked me, lighting a cigarette of a foreign brand.

'I am already doing a job. It is quite good,' I replied.

'Quite, quite. But still, you are a sharp young man. You should do something more. Try to get a foreign degree in management or whatever. Nowadays, a simple graduation won't get you too far. The times are changing,' Mr Malhotra said. He might have been sincere in his advice. Riya looked up towards me.

I knew that Mr Malhotra knew perfectly well the amount of money he was shelling out to pay for Riya's studies and living in the USA, and also that I could not afford it. Maybe, he was thinking about me applying for and getting some scholarship.

But I really didn't want to study abroad. I was not sure if the academics of social sciences and management which they taught in foreign universities, would be relevant in Indian contexts. And also I thought that Indian students, Riya included, were motivated to go and study abroad mainly to see and live a different life, a more convenient and moneyed one, and to eventually settle down in the so-called 'first world'. I didn't want to live abroad, leaving my country, my family, and friends, permanently. But I was not so lucid in my thinking, or confident of my views and didn't want to appear overtly judgemental. So I kept quiet.

Riya expected a response from me and so did her parents. They must have been disappointed at my silence. They even might have thought my silence to be a sign of my stubbornness or even my rudeness. But it was not meant to be.

'I think you need to get some ambition, some drive in you, young man. You tend to get satisfied too easily, too early. Typically middle class characteristics, I may add,' Mr Malhotra said with a slight frown, exhaling the perfumed smoke.

I wanted to correct him that what he actually meant was 'middle income group' and not middle class, but I thought that it would be considered rude. He was speaking in the same language as Riya had, only a couple of days ago. Was it Mendel's law of genetics—similar views germinating in similar environs—or pure coincidence, I didn't know. But I knew that I didn't like Riya speaking and behaving like Mr Malhotra.

'Yes, Sir. Maybe you are right,' I replied, looking at Riya. I didn't relish the direction that the conversation was heading to and I hoped my acceptance of Mr Malhotra's judgement would end it. I was right. It did. At least, on that Christmas evening.

The Malhotras had put up a Christmas tree that year, in their courtyard. It was decorated with a stream of tiny, multi-coloured electric lights. In my childhood, the Christian families of our neighbourhood would put up paper board stars, with an electric bulb lit inside, in their porticos or balconies, to herald the advent of Christmas. Even after Christmas had gone, these stars would stay on till one night the bulbs would stop working and one day the star would vanish, till next Christmas when its successor would take its place. Then, Christmas, for us Hindu kids, meant occasionally visiting the local church, if it was not too far away, to witness the various scenes from nativity play being enacted in their open courtyards—models made up of clay, paper, and thermocol, as well as little dolls showing the scenes of Jesus's birth. Riya's father had arranged for a Christmas cake to be prepared too and a roast chicken to go along. Namrata—their young, teenaged maid servant—brought in the plates of food on a tray, along with tea.

Now that my future was no longer the subject of discussion, the conversation had lost its ebb and we—Mrs Malhotra had also joined us—drank tea in near complete silence, interrupted occasionally by the sounds of spoons clashing with plates and cups. Nobody felt particularly inclined to make small conversation. I noticed, for the first time, that Riya had got her hair streaked in shades of different colours.

32

'So, how was your Delhi visit?' Kajal asked me. We were once again sitting in the now familiar drawing room of Kajal's house.

'It was nice,' I replied. I had returned to Jamshedpur the previous evening. It was New Year's Eve and most of my hostel mates had gone to the company club to celebrate the inevitable arrival of the 'happy' new year. Over the years, the celebrations surrounding the advent of new year have moved on from family bedrooms and 'Doordarshan' television programmes to parties in clubs, hotels, and restaurants with their special, and much flaunted events. But in those days, the expensive tickets, the dancing shows of models and starlets, and the social pressure of being 'seen' had not yet arrived. Although bachelors, living in hostels, would inevitably and naturally, go to clubs to celebrate new year with friends and colleagues over a couple of drinks and what went as dance but it was really alright if one decided to spend a quiet evening at home.

'Has Mr Kulkarni gone to the New Year's party at the club?' I enquired. I had not seen Kajal's father that evening although he had been very much there in the office, earlier in the day.

'Baba never goes to these parties. At least, since I can

remember. Not for any ideological reasons though. He must have gone over to Subhash Uncle's place,' Kajal replied. Subhash Chandra was another colleague of ours, who worked in the same department, and was of Mr Kulkarni's vintage. The two got on well. The families lived in the same neighbourhood, and that helped.

'Let me get something for you. You must be hungry after office,' Kajal decided, without asking, and got up to go to the kitchen. Although I was not particularly hungry, I didn't object and followed her up to the doorsteps of her kitchen. Even though I was not wearing shoes and the kitchen was extremely spacious, still, something stopped me from following Kajal inside.

Kajal started preparing some 'jhaal muri'—a spicy concoction of rice puffs, spices, green chillies and mustard oil, and pakodas—deep fried vegetables in batter of chick pea flour. Our conversation went on as Kajal cut the vegetables.

'Did you go to GSS in between? How is Nirmaladi?' I asked.

'Yes. I have been to Laldih twice while you were not here. Nirmaladi is fine in a usual sort of way,' Kajal replied.

I would have liked to hear that I was missed during my absence, by GSS volunteers, by the villagers, by Nirmaladi, and by Kajal. But there were no such revelations made.

'Doesn't she go out anywhere?' I was curious. 'After all, she has seen the big, wide world. She must be having her friends and acquaintances out there.'

'She does go out, to Kolkata, even to Bombay. Not too frequently though. I guess, now she feels most comfortable in these villages, among these villagers,' Kajal replied, tossing the freshly-prepared jhaal muri expertly.

'I wonder why she didn't get married,' I thought out aloud.

'You are assuming, aren't you, that she is unmarried?' Kajal smiled, looking at me.

'You mean she is married?' I asked, a little surprised. I had always assumed Nirmaladi to be a spinster.

'I am not saying that and frankly, I don't even know. But she might be married, widowed, separated, divorced anything. Even I was married,' Kajal replied.

There was suddenly an awkward silence. Somehow, Kajal's brief marriage with its horribly shocking end, was a topic that used to keep itself out of our conversations. As a matter of fact, I sometimes used to forget that Kajal was ever married, mainly because I had not seen her in the married state. But I think her previous marital status never left Kajal's or her father's mind, for too long.

'I don't know whether I should be asking you this but don't you intend to get remarried, maybe not now, but sometime in future?' I asked, shocked at my own reckless question. Wasn't I being too intrusive?

Apparently, Kajal didn't think so. She reacted quite coolly to my impudent question.

'I think one should marry when one feels very strongly about sharing one's life with another person. Marrying anyone to get married or to be called a married person, somehow, doesn't attract me,' she said.

I noticed that she didn't use the often repeated word 'love'.

'But aren't arranged marriages quite successful, at least in India?' I challenged her theory, although, I had never thought of the possibility of an arranged marriage for myself.

'Look, I am not passing any moral judgement on arranged marriages. They might be very often successful, although it would depend upon how one defines a marriage as successful. I was simply saying what suits me,' Kajal replied. She put some pieces of potato and onion that she had cut into the frying pan. There was a loud hissing sound from the pan as the oil was very hot.

In many ways, I not only found Kajal's views to be very modern and even radical, but also felt that she believed in them truly. Brought up in a relatively small town, cosmopolitan though it was, her not wearing western dresses and jeans had not stopped her from having a truly modern outlook in life, in a quietly confident way. But being convinced of the correctness of her own views didn't make her attempt to hold them up as an universal gospel or to try to convince others about them.

'Right or wrong, arranged marriages are probably the only way to get married in most of India, as boys and girls of marriageable age don't get to meet each other socially, atleast outside the metros. Don't you agree?' I asked, leaning against the kitchen door.

'That I agree,' Kajal replied. 'Why don't you bring a chair from the drawing room, if you have to be here?' Kajal asked, smilingly. Her smile was open and confident and had nothing of the shamefacedness and hesitation that you often see. I noticed that it was very attractive too.

'No, no. It is alright,' I replied, a bit ashamed as if Kajal had detected and questioned my desire to be at the kitchen doorstep, which she had decidedly not. 'Even you are standing, aren't you?'

'Yes, but I had not gone to office,' Kajal smiled again.

'Anyway, I am almost done here. Let me make the tea, and then we can go and sit in the drawing room.' She put the water to boil. Kajal never boiled the tea leaves along with water, I had noticed earlier too. The tea leaves were always added later to the hot water in the tea pot and given time to impart their flavour.

Mr Kulkarni entered, just as we, Kajal and I, sat down again in the drawing room. He folded the umbrella carefully in the porch, before entering the drawing room. I had not noticed that there had been an unseasonal rain outside, which could be called heavier than a drizzle. Maybe the sound of frying had obscured the sound of raindrops falling.

'You are just in the right time—JIT, as they say in Japan,' I remarked, welcoming Mr Kulkarni in his own house.

Mr Kulkarni smiled genially and genuinely, but shaking his head, declined. 'No, no. I have had my dinner although it was rather early. But Subhash's wife wouldn't let me go without food, as always. I will go inside and change. You enjoy the snacks and tea.' Mr Kulkarni almost hopped inside, careful not to wet the durrie that was on the floor of the drawing room.

'This rain is going to make it colder. As such this winter has been unusually cold. But, of course, you wouldn't feel it too much. You are, after all, a Delhiwallah,' Kajal said, putting the plates, bowls and cups on the low centre table.

Somehow, I didn't like being called a 'Delhiwallah,' not because I was ashamed of having lived my childhood and early youth in Delhi but because the term didn't imply too many positive connotations. The connotations associated with a word or phrase are more important than their literal meanings. But I didn't object, not only because I didn't know what was I if I was not a 'Delhiwallah'—but more so because by that time, I knew Kajal was incapable of pettiness and that she had not implied anything more than the fact that I had lived in Delhi.

33

It was a Sunday, a holiday for me. But many of my colleagues, including my roommate, had gone to the factory. The factory was kept open all week during high demands. The weekly offs of workers and officers in Production and Maintenance departments were staggered so that it could operate every day. In service departments like mine, we always had our weekly offs on Sundays like 'normal' offices. Although, that in itself was a source of envy for many in 'line' departments but nobody wanted to join a 'service' department instead of the 'line' one. I was, however, not only always glad to have my rare holidays from the monotonous office work, but also I especially relished Sundays like these when I could enjoy the silence and solitude of my room.

It was an especially cold winter day. The windows of my first floor hostel room were barred but there were no curtains. In those days, only the rooms on the ground floor used to have strictly functional and Spartan curtains. Curtains as an object of beauty never entered our male, bachelor minds.

I lay on my cot, gazing at the ceiling, trying to think. I had declined Kajal's offer to accompany her to the GSS villages that Sunday. Not that I didn't want to go and meet

Nirmaladi or to accompany Kajal, especially since I had
not met Nirmaladi since I had returned from my short
Delhi trip. For one, I was physically tired, a rarity, but also
I wanted some time and space to myself. I wanted to find
out what I wanted to do with my life, my present, and my
possible future. But now that I had the time and opportunity
to do so, I found my mind wandering in all directions. I
found myself missing company, human voices, and my
hostel mates. I started regretting my decision to say no to
Kajal. I even started feeling guilty about not going to GSS.
I still took my occasional involvement in the workings of
GSS as pleasant 'passtime', but slowly expectations had
risen in the minds and hearts of the simple villagers, who
were not hesitant to articulate them, and maybe even in
the minds of Nirmaladi and Kajal. I didn't know where I
stood in relation to GSS. I didn't know where I stood with
respect to Kajal, and I no longer knew where I stood in
relation to Riya. The last one was difficult to admit. The
truth is that I felt that I didn't know where I stood and
what I stood for. I wanted to clear the cobwebs in my mind
but it was not easy. The mind itself, it seemed, had become
a spider.

I decided to write a leisurely letter to Riya. Our letters
had lately become efforts to discharge responsibilities, to
keep up a custom and to mark our commitments. But I was
no longer sure whether Riya would understand my abstract
dilemmas or shrug them away as esoteric luxuries of an idle
mind, as further signs of my laziness and lack of ambition.
I found myself struggling to put my foggy thoughts on
paper and the letter was left unfinished. I didn't feel like
writing about mundane things like my office work and

colleagues, about whom Riya didn't know, and towards whom she had seldom shown any interest. I slowly began realizing on that cold winter Sunday that I wanted to talk to Kajal, and she seemed to be the only person with whom I could attempt to open up confidently. I realized that from her I would get at least an honest effort to understand, rare empathy, and warmth. It was a revelation to me but the acceptance of the revelation came with a curious feeling of guilt, as if I was betraying the trust that Riya had put in me.

Luckily for me at that very moment, my roommate banged open the doors and barged into the room along with a gust of chilly air. He had come to the hostel for a brief lunch break.

'Had your lunch? There is chole bhature in the mess today,' he said. 'I am going to wash up quickly and then we can go together,' he offered.

I was glad to rejoin with the external, reasonable world, and to escape my internal one.

'Yes, I was waiting for you only. Let's go. I am feeling hungry too,' I replied, masking my lie effortlessly. Apparently, it didn't show.

34

Vandana, the young woman with dark, oiled hair and a warm, toothy smile, whom I had met on my first visit to GSS villages, used to always giggle at me in a shy sort of way. But she was not her usual sunny and cheerful self the next weekend when I went to Laldih with Kajal. Her face was dark and sunken, and worry had cast a long shadow across it. I had gone to Laldih after quite sometime, in fact, for the first time since I had returned from Delhi. But even Kajal, who had been going to Laldih and meeting the villagers, including Vandana, was initially clueless. Soon, upon enquiry, it was revealed that Vandana's three-year-old daughter, her only one, Mini, had been terribly and suddenly sick since the night before. Nobody could guess why and how she had fallen sick, but Mini had been vomiting and having loose motions, leaving her almost unconscious. On top of it, she had high fever, which made her delirious. I had met Mini a number of times on my previous visits and the transformation of such a lovely and chirpy girl to this half conscious, supine wreck would have been difficult to imagine if I had not witnessed it myself.

Nirmaladi was not in Laldih. She had gone to Calcutta for some work and in her absence, Vandana and the rest of village women were fearing the worst for Mini. The doctor,

Dr Dasgupta, who attended the GSS-run dispensary-cum-clinic, visited the village only on Tuesdays and Fridays, when he travelled from his home in the city. The villagers had no way to reach him, in between the week, in those pre-mobile days. There was a government-run Primary Health Centre at the 'Block' headquarters, a small mofussil town, some twenty kilometres away. But nobody was sure whether there would be any doctor there, especially, as it was a weekend. The next bus scheduled to go to the city was the same one in which I and Kajal usually travelled back in the late evening. It was pretty clear that it would be very unwise to leave Mini unattended till evening. In fact, she needed expert medical help and medicines as soon as possible and something needed to be done quickly. I suddenly found Vandana, and all the other villagers looking up to us, to Kajal and me, with hope, faith, and expectation. But for me, it was much more than fulfilling their hopes or proving myself useful. I had only Mini and her sunken face in my mind. I could not let her slip away.

It transpired that although Laldih had no automobile among all the hundred odd families living, in the nearby village of Jhansudih, nearly three kilometres away, a somewhat moneyed villager, owned a tractor and a trolley. I decided to walk—there was no other way—to Jhansudih, with the hope that the tractor trolley would not be out on business. I would try to get its owner to lend it to us for transporting Mini to a city hospital. In the meantime, Kajal, with the help of eager women of the village, had started administering fluids—salty lentil soup—to the half-conscious Mini to get some much needed salts and water back into her weak and dehydrated body. Wet bandages—

strips of old, worn cloth dipped in water—were applied to Mini's forehead, in an attempt to get her temperature down. There was nothing else that could be done in the village. So leaving Kajal to look after Mini and her much worried mother, I started on my walk towards Jhansudih.

A local youth called Lallan volunteered to accompany me, to show me the way and act as a much needed guide, companion and a go-between. Laldih was situated on a road, that was though not perfectly maintained but nevertheless it was an all weather paved one. But to reach Jhansudih, we were to walk through empty fields as well. As it was winter, all the nearby fields were shorn of crops. Like elsewhere in the entire Chota Nagpur plateau, the farmers in Laldih and in her neighbouring villages could get only one, monsoon-based, rain fed, paddy crop out of the reddish brown soil of their fields, and for the rest of the year, the fields were left barren. The men, mostly tribal, had no farm work to keep them employed for half of the year and they could no longer go to the forests to hunt or collect forest produces as in the time of their ancestors. The forests were now owned and controlled by a distant and invisible government with its local and visible forest guards. So most of them, like Mini's father, would leave their villages to work in the mines and factories of nearby townships or even go to more distant and larger cities like Calcutta and Bombay to earn their living and accumulate precious savings, which they hoped to send back to their families. Lallan told me, on our way to Jhansudih, that Vandana's husband and Mini's father, Raju, had gone to Bombay and was probably working as a construction worker somewhere. Although Raju's letters would occasionally reach his family, there was no way Vandana could reach Raju, even if she needed to, as he had no permanent address in Bombay. But at least, thanks to GSS, both Raju and Vandana had learned to read and write and so Raju had acquired the confidence to fend for himself, alone, in that vast and unknown world.

'Although, everybody would prefer to live in the village, with their families, there is nothing to do here, and one requires money to live. So Raju and others like him, have to go to the cities in search of work and money. I would also go someday,' Lallan told me. We were walking, very briskly, through the empty farmlands of reddish, granular soil, dotted with sharp stubs of the last crop, cut months back. The sky was rather cloudy and the sun was playing an endless game of hide-and-seek. It was not a very long walk and there was no village in between to cross but it didn't appear to be such a short walk either.

'How old are you? Do you go to school?' I asked, half out of curiosity and half out of politeness.

'I am almost fourteen, I think. I did go to school, the village school, and can read and write. But now I don't go to school. The high school is too far away and its expensive,' Lallan replied.

'I thought there was a government high school in the nearby block headquarters which provided almost free education?' I enquired further, suspecting the genuineness of Lallan's plea, in my ignorance.

'There is. But one has to pay for uniform, books, copies, pens, and pencils. It costs money. Only a few boys from the village go there. Also, if I go to attend the school, who would do all the household work at home? My father is too old now and has no strength left in his bones,' Lallan explained.

After that, our conversation gradually died out till the roofs, thatched and tiled with local reddish mud tiles, of the distant huts of a village appeared at a distance.

'We have reached,' announced Lallan, although I had suspected the same.

35

Luckily for us, the owner of the tractor, one Rahman Mian, a comparatively well off and therefore respected villager, a so-called important man in the village, happened to be at home, that Sunday. Although Lallan knew the way to Jhansudih, once inside the village, even he didn't know the way to Rahman Mian's house as he had never actually been there earlier. He asked a local boy, half naked and staring at us, having interrupted his self-absorbed amusement.

'Which is the way to Rahman Mian's house?' Both the language and tenor were quite different from what Lallan had been using with me.

The boy pointed us to a white-washed brick building at a short distance, probably the only pucca building in the village, at least as far as I could see. But in addition, just to make sure that we went our way, or maybe simply for amusement, he ran in front of us, barefeet, till we reached Rahman Mian's house and then quietly and expectantly stood a little distance away, staring at the proceedings with obvious curiosity. Rahman Mian, clad in his once white vest and blue striped lungi—a cloth, worn wrapped around from waist downwards, a kind of sarong—was sitting in front of his house, on a cot, apparently, idling away his time when we approached him with our request. To my utmost relief, the tractor and also the trolley were visible to us, parked in the open space, a little distance away. This time I started the conversation, hoping that it would have greater chance of success and fearing that the old man, as Rahman Mian quite clearly was from the colour of his beard, would not take Lallan, barely a teenager, seriously enough.

'We are coming from the nearby village of Laldih. A small girl there is very ill and needs to be taken to the city for treatment urgently. We have come here to request you to lend your tractor, and trolley so that we can take her to hospital,' I said. I hoped that the old man understood what I was trying to convey. I felt unsure about whether I should add any offer of money to my request. Lallan sat nodding his head in silent approval of what I was saying.

'How will you take it? Who will drive?' Rahman Mian asked suddenly. It was the first time he spoke since our arrival. His voice was heavy, layered with experience and laboured, but not unkind. It was the most obvious question in the situation, but in the anxiety and hurry, I had not given any thought to this essential question. I had not sat on a tractor ever in my life, let alone drive one, that too on a highway. I looked at Lallan who was staring at Rahman Mian, maybe in order to avoid my eyes.

Suddenly Rahman Mian shouted at some invisible man in the house behind him. Before I could understand his import, a young man, almost my age, bronzed and muscular, wearing a much whiter vest than Rahman Mian's, and a lungi, supporting an impressive moustache, emerged from the darkness. He looked at Rahman Mian with a mixture of enquiry and deference. Rahman Mian explained in his local dialect something to the young man, who was, from his remarkable resemblance in physical features, quite clearly his son. I could not understand the whole thing but it was clear that Rahman Mian was trying to help us. He asked his son, Yunus, to get ready, and quickly to drive the tractor trolley, to transport Mini to a city hospital. As he despatched his son, inside to get ready, he shouted once more in the same direction, to someone else to bring some water and jaggery. He asked me to sit and rest on the charpoy that was laid down opposite him, till Yunus got ready.

I felt relieved and a bit uneasy at the same time as I sat on the charpoy opposite Rahman Mian. Relieved that we had got hold of the tractor trolley for which we had come to Jhansudih at the first place, and that we would now be able to transport Mini to the city and to safety. But I didn't know how to offer money to Rahman Mian for the rent or for the diesel of the tractor. I didn't want to err either way in such delicate a situation. Rahman Mian, in his own nonchalant but charitable way, solved my dilemma. He looked at me and said, 'Babu, there is not much diesel in the tractor or in my house, at this moment. So when you go towards the city, fill the tank up, on the highway— there is a petrol pump on the way, Yunus would know. That would do. You can leave the tractor when you reach the city hospital. Yunus will drive it back. May god be with you and the little, suffering girl.'

I made a feeble attempt to thank Rahman Mian that appeared, even to my ears, as superfluous and unnecessary, and that Rahman Mian quickly brushed aside. Presently, a young woman emerged from the darkness behind Rahman Mian, with a long veil made up of an end of her saree, drawn over her face all the way down to her chin, carrying three stainless steel tumblers, and a small bowl with some dark brown jaggery and moist chick peas—all balanced on a large stainless steel plate—that acted as a serving tray, she put them in front of us, on the cot on which Rahman Mian was sitting. I imagined her to be Yunus's wife but I could have been totally wrong. The silent, veiled woman, invisible in her saree, vanished back into the darkness that was her home. Rahman Mian handed me a glass tumbler and the bowl of jaggery and enquired about my real antecedents as it was obvious that I, with my jeans, sneakers and tee shirt, language and diction, and other worldliness, didn't belong to Laldih. As I answered, from the corner of my eye, I could see an aeroplane, moving across the clear sky, at a height so enormous that it appeared to be completely silent and only its whitish grey exhaust, making a clear straight line against the blue, which gave away its presence.

36

That night, I stayed at the city hospital and returned to my hostel only the next morning. By that time, Mini was completely out of danger, and Yunus had gone back after having been thanked profusely by all. A smile of relief had at last re-emerged, tentatively as if she was afraid to smile too early, on Vandana's face. I had insisted on Kajal's returning home the previous night and independent-minded that she was, she acceded to my insistence on the condition that she would return to the hospital early in the morning. Then I would retire to my hostel to rest and that I would take leave from my office the next day. The hospital was large, clean, spacious, and seemed efficient, with white uniformed nurses, and young, fresh faced doctors, going about their duties in white-walled wards, and corridors with an air of duty and assurance. The hospital was run by the company and I had feared that it catered to only its own employees and their families. But they had admitted Mini the previous day on my recommendation without asking too many questions, and apart from the odd medicine that I had to buy from the shop across the street, no fees or money had been required. I had spent the entire night, sitting on one of the straight-backed, stiff plastic chairs which were securely fixed to the walls of the long corridor, outside the ward where Mini lay recovering, thankfully. It was a case of simple but acute gastric infection, and she had responded to the medicines, that were administered through the drip by the matronly-looking efficient nurse. The nurse, from her appearance and her diction, appeared to have come from Kerala, to this steel city to earn her livelihood in this noblest of professions. The night had been cold, long, and silent. I felt tired and stiff, and yet was satisfied, relieved, and even a little proud of having done something good and noble— all mixed together in a way that defied precise definition in words.

In the early morning, barely at daylight, Kajal along with her kind father, came to the hospital to enquire about Mini and also to bring my breakfast, providing me with an opportunity to retire to my hostel.

'Mini is safe and has recovered quite well. She is sleeping peacefully at present,' I informed them without being asked. 'You need not have bothered to come so early,' I added.

Mr Kulkarni just smiled in a disarming way as was his habit while Kajal quietly pushed the breakfast, packed in a polythene bag, bearing the name of a well-known sweet shop in the city, towards me.

'Now, you go and take rest. I am here. Anyway, Mini is now better,' Kajal said with a touch of concern in her voice that appeared rather satisfying to my ears.

'I will but I think I should hear what the doctor has to say in his early morning round. He should be here soon,' I replied.

We all settled down in the vacant chairs to wait for the

doctor. Mr Kulkarni, it appeared knew the doctor. Dr Mukherjee was young, had recently passed out from Calcutta Medical College, efficient, and quite clearly shouldering a heavy workload. He reassured us that Mini was indeed fine and the hospital should be relieving her the next morning itself. Mini's now peaceful and serene head lay bordered with her jet black hair that formed a halo against the white pillow of her hospital bed. Her breath was steady and deep, and the colour had returned to her cheek.

As I took leave to return to my hostel, Vandana touched my feet with her hand in a sudden and heartfelt expression of 'pranam'—a traditional gesture of deep respect and almost reverence shown to elders. Her voice was heavy and layered with deep emotion as she said, 'Dada, if it had not been for you, I shudder to think what would have happened to Mini. You are like god to us.'

I didn't know how to react and tried ineffectually to show polite humility, and negate my role in the whole affair. But deep down, I knew that Mini had been saved that day by a combination of many fortuitous circumstances. If it had not been a Sunday, if I and Kajal, had not gone to Laldih on that very day, if Rahman Mian or Yunus or their tractor had not been in their village that day, and if they had not been so generous, or even if my company had not decided many decades ago to build and run this excellent hospital which they were not obliged to, either by law or by common business management principles, it could have been a very different morning for Mini or Vandana. For the first time since I had taken up my job, I felt proud to work for my company. I felt a part of a great and noble purpose coming to action all around us and I felt that even my mundane job of drawing jigs and fixtures, which I had thought so lowly about, was a part of something far bigger and nobler than I had ever imagined. It was with these thoughts on my mind, that I returned to my hostel room and fell asleep, almost instantaneously. All the hidden tiredness of the previous twenty-four hours flooded in together and enveloped me, and I drifted away even before doing justice to the breakfast that Kajal had so lovingly made for me, so early in the morning.

37

A strong and beautiful golden thread of love bound Kajal and Mr Kulkarni, that was rare even between a father and daughter. Maybe, it had been caused by the absence of Kajal's mother in their lives, or it might have been a comparatively recent phenomenon occasioned by the recent tragedy of Kajal's short-lived marriage. But regardless of its source, their mutual love and faith filled their house with a sense of peace and happiness that strove to drive away the memories of the tragic past. More than Kajal, it was Mr Kulkarni who had grown to depend on his daughter, less physically than otherwise, to the extent that in Kajal's absence, the house seemed empty, and moments unmoving to him.

I found him in such a state of mind that Saturday, when I arrived at their house in the evening. In those days when phones were still rare, and mobiles were yet to appear, going to somebody's home unannounced was neither uncommon nor was it taken amiss by anyone. Mr Kulkarni was sitting beside the window of his drawing room, on a low chair, with an open book on his lap. But if he was absorbed in his reading and was disturbed, it didn't seem to be, as he welcomed me so warmly and openly that it would have bordered on enthusiasm, had it not been tinged with a rare sense of gloom. I didn't know how exactly, but one step into the house, one look around the drawing room, and there was nothing seemingly out of place that I could detect, and I knew that Kajal was not at home. The house appeared to be different, silent, dark, brooding, and the air was still and suspended.

'Kajal has gone out. She should be back in sometime,' Mr Kulkarni informed me, resuming his seat, knowing quite rightly that I had mainly come to meet Kajal. But in reality, I respected Mr Kulkarni a lot and liked his company. Although we shared the same office space, that didn't offer meaningful conversations, which can be carried on between two individuals, beyond the most mundane.

'No. That is fine. Although I was expecting her,' I replied.

The conversation, as it usually happens, started with everyday topics like the weather, work, colleagues, and the like, till it gathered the strength and confidence that allows any conversation to move into areas more intimate or profound.

'Do you sometimes think about Kajal's future? I mean, she should be marrying again and settling down, no?' Although I had become quite close to Mr Kulkarni's family, I surprised myself by asking such a direct question, which appeared to me, once spoken, as going into areas that were too personal, and probably too painful. But the words had already left my lips.

There was a blank silence. Mr Kulkarni appeared to be composing his thoughts before uttering them into a response.

'Naturally, I want Kajal to be happy, now and always. I

think it would be natural and the right course if she marries again, a person who would deserve her and make her happy. But I don't want to push her about marriage or about any other thing. If she is destined to be happy, she would be,' Mr Kulkarni replied. He added, 'We are not as powerful to decide our future, though we think we are.'

It was a sad reflection and acceptance of the recent and sudden tragedy that had struck the family.

'Knowing Kajal's devotion to such lofty ideals, it is difficult to get to meet such men, at least, in today's age,' I said as if I was pretty knowledgeable in such matters.

'Why, Kajal thinks very highly of you, in these matters and otherwise too,' said Mr Kulkarni.

It had been a spontaneous response from him but in the context of the conversation, it made us both feel awkward and there suddenly rose the need to steer the talk to safer harbours.

Luckily, at precisely that point of time, Kajal entered home in a particularly cheerful mood.

'It is very pleasant outside. It is cold but then at this time of the year, that is how it should be. The air is crisp and fresh, and there is a lovely breeze,' Kajal announced as she smiled at us and took her place on a settee. 'How long have you been here?' she asked, looking at me.

'Not very long. But I and Kulkarniji were enjoying our chat, I guess,' I answered. It struck me that we were unnecessarily thinking and discussing about Kajal's future since she appeared to be completely happy and content with her life presently. In fact, despite her tragedy, she seemed to be more at peace with herself and with her life, than, say, I was.

'And what were you talking about?' Kajal asked innocently, this time looking at both me and her father. She appeared to be honestly curious and I don't think she suspected that we were talking about her life and future.

'Generally. About life, about future.'

This time it was Mr Kulkarni who spoke before I could bring myself to answer, clearly avoiding to reveal that Kajal was the subject of our discussion.

'Let us live fully in the present and try to do our best now. The future will take care of itself. And even if we think and talk, and worry about future too much, it doesn't really help much, does it?' Kajal announced. 'At least, that is what I think.'

'If everybody starts thinking like you, insurance companies and provident funds would cease to exist,' Mr Kulkarni laughed.

'I think, the essence is balance. Practically, one can't afford to really ignore the future completely or refrain from planning for it. But it should not be done so excessively that one forgets to enjoy and work in the present. And I think that is what Kajal meant,' I said, trying to defend Kajal's statement, and I meant what I said.

'Thank you. You are right and that is why one forgets to enjoy the daffodils, or in our case the roses. And Pankaj babu, although you are good in theorizing, but it is you who always dwell on the past or on the future at the expense of the present, as I have often noticed myself,' Kajal said, smiling, while getting up. It was the first time she had used the suffix 'babu' with my name.

I too rose to leave. It was getting late and I didn't want to make it a habit of having my meals at Mr Kulkarni's place. Despite the obvious and visible warmth with which I had always been welcomed at their place, much more than at any other house in my life, I could not bring myself to assume things unhesitatingly. I was always afraid of being accused of piling on even if there was no real likelihood of that.

38

Although Riya neither spoke about it in as many words on any of our meetings on our vacations in Delhi, nor did she ever write clearly about it, her letters gave me an impression that she was mentally prepared to stay in the USA for a long haul or even forever. She seemed to be so totally and happily engrossed in her University, in her colleagues and in her activities that it didn't seem probable that Riya would come back very soon if she had any choice about it. Her parents, although they loved her in their own way, also wanted Riya to continue living in USA. She had, by that time given up finally, on convincing me to go to USA to study, by appearing for exams, and applying for scholarships, as so many of my colleagues and hostel mates were busy doing. It seemed to be such a natural choice that I don't think they ever even thought about it as one. It appeared to them, or so I thought, as a straight path ahead with no possible diversions or cross roads. But as for me, I needed a solid reason to move to a foreign country, and the prospects of living in a developed country, having a more comfortable life—it was universally believed to be—and earning more money were no motivations to me, at all. I was indeed curious about the world and wanted to travel and learn about the wonders of nature and men in god's world. But I wanted to travel, sometimes, as a traveller to those foreign shores, on some vacation, from India. I didn't want to do the reverse. I also felt a sort of responsibility and a vague sort of obligation towards my country, and my countrymen. But I had no idea about what it was and how I could do anything about it. My thoughts also seemed to be too idealistic, too self righteous, and even a bit too naïve to be expressed in front of others, who didn't think like me.

Kajal was almost the only person, I realized, with whom I could discuss these issues, easily and comfortably. The other was Gautam, my colleague and hostel mate. Gautam, like a few others in the hostel, was preparing for the civil services examinations, to get into the Indian Administrative Services, the IAS, the premier civil service of the country. It is a historic successor of the India Civil Services that the British had created to make a band of officers—then almost wholly British—to administer the country and help formulate policies. Gautam was clear, or so we both believed, about what he wanted to do. He wanted to join the IAS to serve the country and his countrymen, and he was quite honest and motivated about it. I suspected he was an exception in this, as the others wanted to join the services because of the status, esteem, and glory associated with them and sometimes to fulfil expectations of their families, who wanted to see their academically brilliant children fulfil their unfulfilled dreams. Gautam was not like that and was preparing for the exams—one of the most competitive in the world—to work for the betterment of people. But the facet of heroism of the act must also have somewhat motivated him. In this, he was, I thought, somewhat similar to Nirmaladi. His positive attitude and motivation was contagious but I realized, early enough, that as far as I was concerned, it was impossible to work in the factory and at the same time prepare for the exams. The task seemed too daunting, too uphill, and frankly I was not as strongly motivated about public service as Gautam was. Other motivations didn't affect me—not strongly enough to drive me enough to try. The exams seemed to be testing a candidate's degree of motivation to join the services rather than his aptitude for the same, but it could not, or possibly couldn't have, ascertained the source of that motivation. There I thought a problem lay.

'Do you think you can really clear the exams? You hardly get any time to study, with these long factory hours of work. And you are competing with all those Delhi University types, who don't do anything except study to prepare for this exams, year after year, at the cost of every distraction. I have seen some of them myself, during my college days,' I told Gautam. We were sitting on the paved banks of the Dimna Lake, a huge artificial reservoir that supplied water to the factories and residential colonies of the town.

'I don't know. But I would never find out if I don't try, would I? I can't leave my job and study as your friends in Delhi. I have to send money home, every month to help my parents. So the question doesn't arise, does it?' Gautam had a peculiar way of talking, putting up rhetorical questions to emphasize his statements, questions that neither expected nor usually were answered.

'I really wish you luck but I think, at least when I look at myself, that it is almost impossible. It is almost futile,' I answered.

'Let's see how it goes,' Gautam threw a small, flat piece of tile on the surface of the water, slinging his arm. The tile bounced on the surface, twice or thrice, while travelling a long distance before taking the inevitable and final plunge. I didn't know whether Gautam was talking about the piece of tile or the exams.

'I don't want to grow old and later repent and regret that I didn't try honestly for something that I really wanted to do. I don't want to live and die with regret in my heart. I have seen my father, who after clearing the written exams, simply didn't go to attend the interview for the selection to the Indian Airforce as a pilot. To this day, he imagines about the life of a pilot, that could have been his, especially when a jet plane is seen in the sky,' Gautam spoke after the piece of tile had vanished from our view. I knew then that he was talking about the exams. I admired his approach to life, motivation, integrity, and his single-mindedness. I wished him success in his path, from the bottom of my heart, silently. But it was his path, not mine.

The sun was setting. Gautam and I had wanted to visit this lake, early in the morning to look at the sunrise, which was said to be very beautiful. Although Gautam was up and about, I couldn't bring myself to wake up, despite the alarm clock, so early in the morning on the only weekly off day. Therefore, we had come in the afternoon.

A few families were enjoying their day out on the banks of the reservoir, and were now packing up their tiffin carriers and straw mats. There were a few couples, apparently in love, sitting at further corners, seeking space and privacy. Whole flocks of geese and other unknown birds flew across the sky, over the lake, maybe, to their homes. Another day had passed, another day less in our lives on the planet, but I was sure that nobody except me, on the banks of Dimna Lake that day, realized it in quite the same way.

39

'Vandana has asked me to especially request you to visit their village this Sunday. There is some sort of celebration there, an annual festival. Of course, Nirmaladi would also be very happy to see you, as you know,' Kajal remarked.

We were sitting in the dining hall of the Officer's Club, which was run and managed by the company for its officers. It was the only place for entertainment in a radius of fifteen kilometres. The only other option to go out occasionally, with friends, was riding our two wheelers for some twenty kilometres, to one of the few restaurants or cinema theatres that were all in the heart of the city. It was this singular lack of any other place and not so much its impressively maintained premises and lawns, or its sporting facilities that drove some officers—especially the ones who liked their drinks—to the club in the evenings, and especially to its bar and dining hall. We were however rather early and till then alone.

'Yes. I want to go too. Even last Sunday, I had wanted to go to Laldih but just couldn't manage,' I replied.

There was actually no need to explain to Kajal and she very well knew that suddenly there had been excessive work load in the office last week, to deliver some drawings within a short and fixed deadline. That had kept both me and Mr Kulkarni crouched over our drawing boards, in the deserted and silent office. Indeed, it was Kajal who had brought home-made food for both of us to the office, as we had got late.

'Yes. I know but Nirmaladi and GSS have started depending on you. They really look forward to your visits and everytime I travel alone, nowadays, I am met with eager, expectant faces, which are disappointed. They never waited for me that much,' Kajal chuckled, lightheartedly but warmly.

Ricky and Gurusahay, my colleagues and hostel mates, had peeked into the dining hall, on their way to the bar. They avoided us, although we were not exactly invisible to them. They were still in their office uniforms and apparently on their way back from office to hostel.

'I sometimes feel guilty, as I have told you earlier also, about taking on responsibilities of GSS, and yet not being able to spare the time and effort to fulfil them,' I told Kajal. The uniformed waiter had brought the two cups of milky coffee that we had ordered and kept them on the white-topped table that separated me and Kajal.

'Don't worry. Those people don't wait for you because of the work that you help them with, not that it is not important, but they look forward to your visits anyway. And this time Vandana's husband Raju has come from Bombay, and Vandana wants him to meet you,' Kajal said.

'Is it? I will try to make it this Sunday, definitely then,' I replied. We both knew that her father, Mr Kulkarni was my boss, but we also knew equally clearly that as far as office was concerned, there was no question of me asking any favour or allowance from him. Although I suspected that if ever I could bring myself to indulge in such an act, it would have been difficult for Mr Kulkarni, the generous spirit that he was, to refuse my request.

The winter had lost its teeth and yet there was still a nip in the air which was quite nice and crisp. The Indian spring is very brief and arrives very early, in late February, and departs even earlier and sooner than one realizes. Then the sky turns into a hot luminescent plate and the rows of gulmohur trees, lining the road that leads upto the Officer's Club, bloom with their profuse, reddish-yellow blossoms.

On our way out, I somehow felt obliged to make a short detour to the bar, to greet Ricky and Gurusahay, who behaved as if they had not noticed us previously, but were not very good in their pretence. I introduced Kajal to them as Mr Kulkarni's daughter, unconsciously and unnecessarily explaining my association with her. Kajal was wearing a pair of jeans that day, the first time I had seen her in western clothes, and seemed somehow younger than usual when she wore her simple, plain cotton sarees. Ricky and Gurusahay, neither being very close to me nor belonging to my department, had not heard of Kajal or Mr Kulkarni. They responded warmly enough to my greetings, but were not sure about offering me a stool or a drink as Kajal had accompanied me. The bar was a strictly male bastion in that overwhelmingly male-dominated club. The question of offering Kajal a drink never arose in any of our minds, although I am not absolutely sure now about her. In those days, offering an alcoholic drink to any lady, especially in a public place, in the unlikely event of it ever happening, was sure to be considered a deliberately rude act.

'Am I only Mr Kulkarni's daughter and is my father your boss only?' Kajal asked me, getting on the rear seat of my scooter, in the parking lot. I didn't know how serious she was or how concerned she was about my answer as I couldn't see her, while I put the scooter on gear.

'No you are not, and I don't think of you only as Mr Kulkarni's daughter. But that was a convenient way of introducing you to them, I suppose,' I replied. The cold breeze was blowing against my face, under my helmet, on the dark night, as the scooter gained speed on its way to Kajal's home.

'What do you think of me?' I could only barely detect a slight hint of chuckle in Kajal's voice, but I was not sure and I couldn't turn my face while driving to check. I think she realized that. I was not a glib talker and especially when I was not completely frivolous and joking. I didn't know how to respond to Kajal's question. To say that I didn't think of her at all would have been both untrue and rather rude, but to say that I thought about her would also have implied something that would not have been totally true. There was a silent blank. Many minutes passed and the moments and the sound of scooter's engine slowly drowned the question into the dark night, and Kajal didn't repeat her question.

As we reached her home and she got down from my scooter, I managed to look at her face in the light of the yellow bulb that lighted up her doorway. If she had indeed been joking when she had asked me the unanswered question, there was no indication of in her eyes.

'Okay. So do try to manage this Sunday. It would be nice if you can come along to Laldih,' Kajal said.

She waved at me with a smile, as I put my scooter on neutral and turned it around to start.

'Sure. I would. See you then,' I replied amidst the smell of petrol fumes before starting on my way to my hostel. Alone now and therefore driving at a higher speed, I thought whether Kajal wanted me to go to Laldih, solely for the sake of Vandana, Nirmaladi, and her GSS villagers. I found myself wishing that it was not so.

40

It appeared that the village had been specially cleaned and spruced up for the celebrations, although it had been quite clean on other days too. Buntings, made of fresh, shiny, and green leaves of some unknown trees, had been put up in the narrow lanes and doorways of houses. Some people had come from a neighbouring village to play music on their drums, and a sort of wind instrument that I had never seen before. Young boys were taking turns to chase each other, while their parents talked and laughed while drinking a local beer called 'Haria', a kind of lightly fermented rice beer that had already been offered to me. Some of the villagers, Raju among them, had taken upon themselves the roles of organizers and were looking busy and important. But otherwise the results of their actions and efforts were not much visible.

Kajal and I had arrived at Laldih in the morning, on that Sunday. I had been able to manage my work during the week and anyway there had not been a tight schedule to follow this time, as on the previous weekend. Nirmaladi, in her white, blue-bordered cotton saree, wrapped in a bluish grey shawl, was sitting in a corner on a sort of settee. She was the centre of almost universal respect and reverence among the villagers, who knew, admired, and loved her.

Kajal and I sat near her, almost as honoured guests of the village, although Kajal knew almost all of them intimately enough. The celebration was an annual custom and an occasion of worship of the village deity that was accompanied with the sacrifice of a game animal that had been hunted in the nearby forests. Over the years, animals fit to be hunted had dwindled in the adjoining forests, and the forest laws and their implementation regarding prohibition of hunting wildlife had become stricter. Hence, on many years, as that one, a domesticated goat was sacrificed instead. The food—simple rice and meat—was being prepared in huge cauldrons in the open, amidst music that seemed to my unaccustomed ears as a sort of peculiar noise. Unlike usual days when the women folk prepared the family meals on that festive occasion, two muscular and dark-skinned men, with sweat glistening on their arms and bare bodies, were moving ladles in the steaming cauldrons in a way that reminded me of boatmen, wielding ores to steer their boats in a broad and unruly river. It was a luminescent, bright day with a clear blue sky and the sun's rays were pleasantly warm. I was enjoying the peaceful and happy situation, and the activities in the midst of which I had found myself that Sunday. The pleasantness of everything slowly engulfed me.

No man or woman, knows how his or her thoughts actually appear, move into unforeseen areas of their own and then disappear, only to be succeeded by some other unsuspected thoughts. Such random thoughts appear all the more frequently and move waywardly when one is at leisure and not inclined to stress his mind. As I sat there, leaning on the mud-washed wall of the hut behind me, that belonged to Vandana and Raju, for no reason that I can tell, my thoughts wandered away from that peaceful village courtyard, across the blue skies and candyfloss clouds—to Riya and my memories of her. How different our surroundings were and how increasingly different were they becoming. She had written to me in her previous letter, how heavy the snowfall had been that year in her University town. Looking at the warm sun rays and the azure skies, it was difficult to imagine the snow-laden, paved courtyards on which Riya would have been walking, or the grey, heavy skies which she would be looking up to. From the whiff of hot spices drifting from the steaming cauldrons and the surrounding expectant hustle-bustle of the villagers, it was difficult for me to imagine what kind of cold sandwiches and pizza slices Riya must be eating absent-mindedly, busy working on her home assignments, in her organized, neat, and clean surroundings. Although she did write something about her life and activities—like how busy she had become in trying to meet the deadlines of submissions of her numerous essays and assignments, it was becoming difficult to be sure about the accuracy of my imagination about her and her life. The differences in time, space, situations, as well as their perceptions, was quite large, I realized. Even the life that I had known with Riya—our life in Delhi—of our college days, appeared to belong to a different world, miles away from my present state of affairs, and not only from my immediate surroundings that day. It appeared to me, that both Riya and I had moved down some distance along our respective paths, since those days. I don't know whether it was the stupor stimulated by the tumbler of Haria that I had been almost forced to drink, despite its smell that was leading to persistently clear thoughts in my mind that Sunday. But at that moment, my self-imposed stupor was broken by Mini.

'Kaku, the food is ready. Baba has asked you to come, all of you,' she said. Mini had started calling me 'Kaku', literally meaning father's younger brother but actually signifying nothing more than a honorific way to address a respected elder. However, her use of the word 'Baba', meaning father, to refer to Raju, was more particular and exclusive. She was wearing a bright pink cotton frock that I could safely assume, had been brought by her father from Bombay.

'New frock? It is very beautiful and suits you too,' I said, appreciating her new dress, more out of a desire to let her know that I had indeed noticed it. This made her immensely and visibly happy, as I had wanted.

'Yes. It is nice, isn't it? Baba has brought it for me, from Bombay,' Mini proudly proclaimed as she showed off her frock for us.

I could see her father, the object of her pride and adulation. Raju walked up to us, wearing his faded yellow cotton shirt over trousers, a rarity in the village. He beamed a shy grin as he repeated the invitation that her daughter had already conveyed on his behalf, a few minutes earlier.

'The food is ready. Come, the villagers are all waiting eagerly for you. Although it is nothing very special—just simple village food,' Raju said, looking from me to Kajal, and to Nirmaladi. I noticed that he addressed the people as villagers as if he was no longer one of them, although I don't think he or anybody else noticed it.

'Yes. I was eagerly waiting too,' Nirmaladi replied,

smiling, getting up and rearranging the folds of her saree. She had known Raju for years and clearly he felt much more comfortable with her than with Kajal and, especially, me.

41

The food, on that occasion of celebration in Laldih, on that lazy blue Sunday, was remarkably hot, spicy, and tasty. The fare was limited, the ingredients known, the cooks unfashionable but the food, at least to my tastes, was delicious in a manner that satisfied without trying to impress. The tumbler of Haria and our previous long wait under the sun had increased my appetite. Although initially I had felt a little stiff and formal, but soon the combined effects of insistence, warmth, hunger, and Haria loosened me up and I found myself eating with my fingers after a very long time. I didn't feel inhibited or self-conscious.

After a stomach full of rich, spicy, and rustic food, I wandered to the outskirts of the village, accompanied by Raju. The empty fields of reddish brown soil stretched in front of us and in the distant haze, I could barely make out the outlines of some clumps of trees and huts, maybe of the neighbouring village, in that direction.

After a little bit of initial hesitation, Raju offered me a cigarette from a packet of Charminar that he took out from a pocket of his trousers. The gesture was friendly enough, but it appeared to me to be too deliberate as if Raju had rehearsed his actions many times earlier in his mind. Though, I normally never smoked in those days—

when smoking had not become so unfashionable and was not considered such a certain cause of ill health as it is now—I didn't want to disappoint Raju. Also I didn't want to be considered a rude and aloof man from the city. After a couple of silent puffs from our respective cigarettes, the conversation started easing a little.

'So, when are you going back to Bombay?' I asked, more out of politeness than any genuine curiosity or concern.

'Maybe after eight or ten days. This time, Lallan has asked me to take him along to Bombay. I might take him with me. Of course, I will have to talk to his old man but I guess, it is best for all concerned. What can he do here, after all? This land can't support us, at least, in today's age,' Raju answered, gesturing towards the bare fields staring at us.

I wanted to ask him about how his life in Bombay was, again less out of concern and more to spend empty moments away, but stopped myself. I was being doubly careful with my words and didn't want to give any occasion of complaint or accusation of being an insensitive, rude, city-bred upstart. But this was more in my mind, I guess, rather than in Raju's.

'I thought you could have invited Rahman Mian and his son Yunus from the neighbouring village for this celebration. It would have been a nice gesture, I guess,' I remarked after a long pause. There was silence and Raju took his time before reacting to my unsolicited suggestion.

'Even Vandana had suggested the same. I admit they were nice in lending their tractor on that day, but I refused to invite them. After all, it is a village affair,' Raju responded, looking towards the distant horizon, taking another long puff at his cigarette.

'But even Kajal and I are outsiders in that sense,' I said.

My response was spontaneous, and to my mind, correct.

'You are different,' Raju replied. I didn't know exactly in what way, he meant Kajal and I were different, and therefore more acceptable than Rahman Mian and his son. Maybe because we were city-bred or because we were more frequent visitors at the village. I thought Raju would turn silent but he was unexpectedly forthcoming.

'These people are different. Although, some of them are kind and nice too.'

It was then that the realization dawned on me that Raju was referring to Rahman Mian's religion. This sort of thinking was entirely unknown to the village, and I thought it was the polluted air of the vicious underbelly of the large city, where Raju was forced to live, that was spoke through his voice.

There had been Hindu-Muslim riots in Bombay a few days back, following bomb attacks on important buildings in the city, which many believed were retaliations against the Babri Masjid demolition, a few months ago. Raju might have witnessed the madness and who knows may have been more than a mere witness. I wanted to refute Raju's obviously wrong contention, but something inside told me that not only would it be futile but would also counter-productive.

Two dark, thin, and gaunt villagers, of some other village, obviously tribals, had suddenly appeared from nowhere and I was a bit taken aback by their sudden presence. They were carrying hand-made tribal bows, made from bamboos, and dangerous looking arrows on their shoulders. This was no longer a common sight, even in tribal villages. One of them looked older, with a grey stubble and a vacant, devout look in his eyes, and was wearing a long, worn out cotton kurta (an Indian long shirt), and dhoti (a piece of cotton cloth worn traditionally to cover the lower part of his body), but only going down as far as his dark knees. The other was younger, more muscular, and wore a red bandana on his forehead. He was chewing betel nuts. It was apparent that Raju knew them and that the duo had been invited to attend the feast. I surmised that Raju didn't consider this tribal duo as sufficiently outsiders. They spoke to Raju briefly but with knowing familiarity in an incomprehensible tribal dialect, exchanging pleasantries, I supposed, before proceeding towards the village.

'They are fighting for our separate state. A state that would belong to us—Jharkhand,' Raju explained, looking at me, after the two men had left us. It was apparent from his manner of speech that Raju clearly believed in the justice and the eventual success of the cause for which his friends were fighting. He looked at me with expectant eyes as if he wanted me to either endorse or challenge his view but I kept silent, this time more out of genuine ignorance rather than politeness. I had only read cursorily a few news items about the movement that used to appear in the local newspapers, whose treatment of the subject was generally superficial, and constrained as their writers compressed age-old, complex phenomena in a couple of columns. Such news, concerning some or the other part of India, keeps appearing in newspapers, jostling with each other, and with advertisements of luxury goods, for limited space and attention. Ultimately, we choose to read in detail only the news that we believe concerns us. I didn't believe, living in the island town of Jamshedpur, that this movement, which occasionally turned violent, concerned the future of the surrounding areas outside the township and its cosmopolitan residents, had even the potential of affecting our daily lives.

'Right now it is only the outsiders who make all the money from our land, our mines, and our forests. We remain the same,' Raju continued explaining his support for the Jharkhand cause as well as trying to provoke a reaction from me. Suddenly I felt distinctly uncomfortable, as if the border of the new state had been drawn on the land that lay between us, separating us. Having failed to elicit any reaction from me, Raju decided that it was time for us to return to the village. We had anyway finished our cigarettes, long ago.

42

For thousands of years, thousands of writers, philosophers and poets, of many different cultures and in various languages, have written millions of words to explain and define love. The wise ones know that all such efforts are futile. Really profound feelings and lofty thoughts can never be explained in words, put within the mortal boundaries made by man's words and earthly reasons.

I no longer knew for sure whether I loved Riya any more, as I had known when we used to meet every day during our time in college in Delhi, before she left me to pursue her studies and her life in the USA. But I was reluctant to admit any such doubts or uncertainty to myself. Whenever any such doubt attempted to raise its ugly head from some unexpected corner of my mind, I would ruthlessly put on a heavy lid of reason, common sense, and certainty over it, and banish it to the darkness. I didn't have the courage to honestly examine whether it was more out of a sense of commitment and loyalty to Riya than to my own imagination that was driving me mad. And although I did have my share of friends, none inspired the confidence that I could share my thoughts with them. But it was not their fault, I didn't dare share my thoughts with even myself. If friendship means spending time in pursuit of a common enjoyment, or in coming to help in time of need, I had many friends in those days. But if it means, and I am not sure that it does, anything more, I had none, in my hostel.

Although I had many so-called friends in my hostel, increasingly it was Kajal with whom I was getting more comfortable, and it was not only because I was increasingly making more frequent trips to GSS villages with her. Each trip gave us almost exclusive time during the long, dusty, and crowded bus journeys that I had come to relish and await. During those long journeys, that didn't appear to be so long then, we discussed almost any topic under the sun—mostly ideas, and events, and rarely even people, from the Jharkhand movement. We talked about things like tribal culture, to the Palestine issue, to religion. But there were two topics that were avoided with a mutual, unspoken agreement—Kajal's past married life and my future with Riya.

'You know, I was thinking for some time to tell you and always hesitated. But consider me a friend when I tell you that you always seem to be a little dissatisfied with the present. There is a little inexplicable restlessness in you. As if, you are waiting for something to happen in future. I can't fully explain it,' Kajal told me one day. It was a little unusual as we rarely discussed each other. Our bus to Laldih had broken down, and we had, along with other passengers, come out of the hot and stuffy bus, and were sitting on a small culvert that bridged a canal that had not seen any water for years, if ever.

Such questions and observations about yourself, deep and honest as they are, are difficult to react to. But I didn't feel uncomfortable with this unwarranted intrusion. Rather it felt nice and warm, thinking somebody had cared to think about me. I didn't know what to say but I didn't want to avoid the subject. I wanted to show Kajal, without saying so, that I was glad that she had cared to observe and think about me with such empathy, but words failed me. I remained silent for a long time but her observations hung in the air surrounding us, waiting for my eventual reaction. The rest of the passengers were loitering nearby, talking to each other. A few were crowding around the hapless driver, who had opened up the engine to try to find out what was wrong with the bus.

'Isn't it so for everybody? Is anybody fully content or satisfied with life?' I finally tried to deflect her observation with a question of my own.

'No, not everybody. You seem to be living always for the future, at the expense of the present. Please don't mind. I have no right to nor am I trying to judge you. It is only as a friend that I observed and you don't like, we can stop,' Kajal offered.

'No, it is alright, really. I do appreciate. Maybe you are right. Subconsciously, I am always trying to search for a higher, greater purpose in my life, something more than what my current life seems to provide. Also, I do feel a bit uncertain about my future, maybe. I don't see a clear picture, for instance, what I would be happy doing ten years from now,' I said.

This time it was Kajal who was silent. But our mutual silence didn't mean lack of communication or understanding. It is rarely that one gets the opportunity and confidence to share such personal and intimate thoughts of oneself as if one is baring oneself, piece by piece, layer by layer, before somebody's patient eyes.

'Maybe, everybody needs to find out answers to such questions by oneself. But not everybody even asks these questions. You are different, in a way,' Kajal remarked after a while. It appeared to be an observation and not a judgement, and I didn't know what she meant exactly when she said I was different. But I was confident that she didn't mean anything disparaging and if anything, she was speaking highly of me. I felt pleased in a very peculiar way.

It appeared that the driver, with his limited knowledge, had given up on repairing the bus, and his helper had been despatched, on foot, to the nearest habitation on the highway to look for a mechanic. The passengers, most of them, had given up their hopes on this bus for the day and were waiting for the next means of transport on the road that would agree to take them at least to the nearest human settlement, if not to their ultimate destination. There was nothing one could do but still there was a remarkable and good humoured acceptance of the situation—no angry quarrels, no show of temper, not even a vociferous complaint, or protest to the driver.

'Do you have answers to your questions?' I asked Kajal, continuing with our conversation, picking up from where it had paused.

'I have learnt not to indulge in too much of long-term thinking,' she said.

It was again a reminder of how unexpectedly her young marriage had ended.

'But I think I am going to immerse myself more fully into the works of GSS and of Nirmaladi. I think there are very few such selfless and purposeful kinds of work, and I feel sort of fortunate about being associated with her,' Kajal replied. 'At least, that is what I think, as of now,' she said.

'That is good. The fact that even a city-bred cynic like me goes back to these villages again and again shows that they are really extraordinary. I too feel fortunate of having being of any use to them, in however small a measure,' I said.

'Actually, as I see it, you are actually doing a lot of useful work, both in your office and by helping GSS. Despite that you feel dissatisfied. Maybe, your sense of uncertainty stems from the fact that you are not entirely sure how and where you and Riya are going to live together. Forgive me if I seem to be meddling,' Kajal remarked.

There was again a long silence. But this time, before I could organize my thoughts sufficiently or arrange my words subsequently, somehow, miraculously our bus, with which our driver had continued to tinker around, came sputtering back to life. We all rushed back to it as if our haste would prevent it from relapsing into the hopeless state from which it had recovered so suddenly. The driver was the man of the moment. He accepted the compliments of passengers with a proud and self-congratulating smile. He resumed the journey and I guess, never dared to stop the engine during the rest of it. Half-way he deposited us at a dusty bend of the road that acted as the bus stop of Laldih.

We didn't follow the conversation any further, but it was not lost, at least on me. Not that I was constantly brooding over such existential questions all the time. The mundane, time-consuming matters of everyday life encroached upon my space and time, as it does, I guess, on everyone's and more so, such questions are uncomfortable and difficult to face.

43

Soon, I was asked by my company to take a trip to Calcutta, in relation to some official work. This was extremely rare as contact with outside world was managed by other departments like Procurement and Marketing. My sedate, cocooned department was rarely, if ever, involved even in any correspondence with vendors, let alone in any face-to-face meetings. But the company, contrary to its old philosophy of doing everything in-house, had started outsourcing many functions—mostly in order to save costs. The jigs and fixtures that Mr Kulkarni and I were drawing, were no longer being manufactured in the shop floors below, but in some distant sheds in the industrial suburbs of Calcutta.

On that occasion, the jigs manufactured by the supplier were not conforming to the specifications, we had designed, despite repeated directions and rejections. As the consequent delay was getting critical, it was decided to send someone from the design team to sort the problem out with the vendor. Because of the heavy work load, Mr Kulkarni could not go himself. So I boarded the Steel Express—the train that brought me from Jamshedpur to Calcutta, one fine morning, after an overnight journey through swathes of darkness, only intermittently being interrupted by dimly lit, small train stations.

I had decided, after consulting Nirmaladi and Kajal, to take advantage of this opportunity that had so unexpectedly come my way to try to build some contacts for the products made by the women of GSS. I carried a few samples in my leather suitcase, along with my clothes and personal belongings. Though Calcutta, once the proud capital of British India and the second largest city of the British Empire, was only an overnight journey from Jamshedpur, I had never visited the city. This was despite the fact that many of my colleagues and hostel mates, who belonged to Calcutta, had repeatedly asked me to accompany them in their frequent weekend trips to their homes. It would appear even more remarkable because my grandmother and aunt lived in Calcutta in the same old house, where my father had spent his childhood and early youth. There was no clear, discernible reason that had stopped me from visiting Calcutta till then, but now, I felt happy and pleased with myself—particularly because I knew that my father, sitting in Delhi, would feel the same at the prospect of me meeting my grandmother, although he had not said anything. Of course, there was no question of my staying in the company guest house, though it was centrally located. I took a black and yellow Ambassador taxi on that cloudy morning to the south of the city, where my grandmother lived with my aunt.

It had been a few years since I had visited them and that house, and it was the first time that I had gone there as a grown up man of independent means and not merely as my father's son. On my mother's bidding, I had bought some gifts, a saree each for my grandmother and my aunt. I knew that although they didn't expect anything, nevertheless it would please them. It was the gesture, more than the gifts, that would be considered valuable—an acknowledgement of a relationship, that they had reasons to suspect, had grown distant over the years. It was something like the proverbial prodigal son coming back home, even if for a couple of days. I had to extricate myself, unwillingly, from the abundant fretting and feeding, that they showered on me, to attend to the vendor, who had sent his car and driver to pick me up.

On the long ride from where my grandmother lived to Howrah, I kept looking out of the open window of the car, taking in the sights, sounds, and smells of the spectacular city, whose streets and lanes appeared familiar from some distant, misty memory. The people on the street corners, the small temples, and the sound of their bells, the white and red saree-clad women with wet hair, the sounds of hawkers and taxis were all familiar, but there was no real memory as I had hardly ever lived there, a city of my father's youth that he left.

44

On reaching our vendor's sheds, I realized that he, Samir, and his expert machinist had managed to rectify the persistent problem themselves, a night ago. The jigs that were being produced by their machine line now were conforming perfectly to our specifications. I satisfied myself and was secretly glad that it was so, as I was unsure, even with all my knowledge of engineering books, if I could have rectified the defect myself. But Samir never made it apparent that my trip had been in vain, and was ever thankful to me to have taken the trouble to visit his humble sheds that doubled up as his office with an air-conditioned cubicle at the corner being used when visitors like me dropped in.

It is to this cubicle that Samir took me. There was a low centre table and a red, velvet-covered sofa set along with his glass-topped office table, and a straight-backed office chair. A dark, teenaged boy took out white china tea cups and saucers from a steel bookcase-type-cupboard as Samir insisted, naturally enough, that I should have at least some tea. In India, tea is hardly ever served to guests without accompaniments and soon the same boy brought in some piping hot samosas from somewhere and poured sweet, milky tea to our waiting cups. A slight drizzle had started outside and the falling rain drops made a pleasant sound on the tin sheets that made the roof. Samir's business had been made from scratch and he was a first generation entrepreneur who had started small with a loan from a government corporation but had grown into what he was today. I admired him and his story.

'It was my good luck and the blessings of Maa Durga. Otherwise I had nothing. No money, no backing, no experience, no political contacts, nothing,' Samir said after we had become somewhat familiar, over a cup of tea. It had not taken us long. It couldn't have been only luck, I was sure. To succeed, he must have had remarkable enterprise, tenacity and worked hard too. Now he was employing more than a dozen workers himself, whereas once he had walked up and down the streets of Calcutta to get a clerk's job in any one of the trading offices, without success.

'Maybe my failure to get an accountant's job was a blessing in disguise. Maybe it is all Maa Durga's wish,' Samir said in his by now familiar, self-deprecating, and god-fearing manner.

'Sir, why don't you take a round of the factory? Maybe you can give me some tips,' Samir requested me as I polished off the last of the delicious samosas. It was after a long time that I had tasted such delicious samosas filled with peas, in addition to the usual spiced potatoes. I didn't know how to react. While I was more than sure that it was beyond me to give any worthwhile advice to this hardworking and worthy entrepreneur, on the other hand, I didn't want to disappoint him or appear to be standoffish. 'Fine, let's go,' I replied.

The shed was around twenty metres long and had a

high tin roof. A few workers were working on ancient looking greasy machines, producing jobs—mainly jigs that would probably and eventually end up in our company. There were noises and smells of an usual busy machine shop—a peculiar sound of machines, shouts, footsteps, and a smell of lubricants, coolants, sweat, and suspended air.

'What's that?' I asked Samir, pointing to a small hand-held tool lying unused, the type I had never seen anywhere before.

'Oh. That is something we make on order. It is a hand-powered machine used to make polythene packets. It is quite useful and high in demand, but right now we are naturally devoting our full attention to the order of your company, since we are already running late. But I assure you we will supply all the jigs within time,' Samir replied. There was a mixture of satisfaction and anxiety in his voice. By this time, his chief machinist Wasim, an old wizened man with grey stubble and dark, weathered skin, had joined us.

'In fact, it was Samir babu who designed it himself. Very useful, especially for small factories who can't afford large electric-based machines. We make and sell them on order,' Wasim pitched in and volunteered to give a practical demonstration of how it actually worked.

I was amazed. Here was a man, educated in conventional college level accountancy, with no professional knowledge of engineering design, but who had come up with something so uniquely useful. I warmly congratulated Samir and asked him about the price for one such machine. My mind was already working on how this could be so useful for the women of GSS.

Samir was puzzled. 'But what would your company do with these cheap, hand-held machines? This is for small concerns, sweet shops, food shops, and the like,' he said genuinely.

'No. It is not for our company. I was thinking of some people I know who may have use of it,' I said.

I told him in a few sentences about the women of GSS, about Nirmaladi's work, and how I had come in touch with them. Somehow I felt that Samir would understand what I was saying. It happens many a time in life that without any apparent explanation, one feels close and resonant with some individual, even on their first meeting. Samir was like that, for me.

'Sir, we sell it for three and half thousand. But for you I would sell it at three thousand, and we can arrange to get it delivered and installed to wherever you want. It would be difficult for you,' Samir replied. He had rightly guessed that left to me, I would indeed find it rather difficult to transport that small but still heavy, steel machine that lay before me.

'You let me know. One of my boys would go and install and train the people too,' Samir added. 'It is good work.'

I don't know whether he meant his own work or that of GSS that I had mentioned.

It seemed to be an excellent offer, and Samir was more than helpful, but I couldn't take a decision on my own, without consulting Nirmaladi. Three thousand rupees was a lot of money. So I took Samir's office phone number and promised to let him know. I already had his postal address.

From the absence of the sound of raindrops on the tin roof, I realized that the rain had petered off. I decided to leave as there was no further occasion or purpose left. We, all three of us, came out as the driver, hardly a youth, who had driven me in the morning went to fetch the car that was parked at some distance. There was no space in the narrow dirt lane in front of Samir's shed for any four wheeler to be parked. A cacophony of sounds was emanating from the different sheds around. From a few, dark smoke was blowing out from chimneys, silhouetted against a sky that was clearing up. A cycle rickshaw with its bells ringing and a boy in dirty shorts passed us by. I bade Samir goodbye as he folded his hands respectfully and smiled, showing a set of sparkling teeth and genuine warmth. I told him that I would get down in central Calcutta somewhere and send the car back.

'No, no sir. Keep it with you. Till the time you are here, the car and the driver would be with you. This is the least that we can do for you,' Samir replied with alacrity as if at last he had found something to do for me, an offer of help that being accepted, provided him with a comfort that had been eluding him till then, despite my verbal assurances.

45

As the car struggled through the wayward and unpredictable traffic over the British-era Howrah Bridge, that spanned over the River Hoogly (the offshoot of the mighty River Ganga), the sun came out from behind the clouds. The river and its banks were suddenly bathed in an ancient light. There were steamers and barges floating along and across the river, with belching smoke overhead. Crowds of commuters rushed towards the jetty at the ferry point in anticipation of the approaching steamers with the resultant, inevitable jostling. At a distance, some women were bathing themselves ritualistically at the banks of their sacred mother river, following some ancient unwritten tradition. Tall chimneys of now defunct jute mills that used to feed on the raw jute grown in the marshlands of East Bengal, now separated by an unanticipated international border, dotted the banks on one side. Those jute barges would never again cross the river and maybe the chimneys had fallen silent, maybe forever. It was a scene out of those watercolour paintings by some itinerant British painters of the last century that adorn exhibitions on the Raj, held both in India and abroad. The sight resonated one of those distant villages, across the border, that my ancestors had come from, and where my roots lay obscured now in some foreign fields, tilled by others, who had once been our neighbours. It was difficult to think.

Although Samir had offered to lend his car for my entire stay in Calcutta, I still felt hesitant. It felt like taking an undue obligation and advantage from somebody, however friendly, with whom I had an official relation. It somehow didn't feel right, in my frame of reference, at that time. So I left the driver in front of Victoria Memorial, despite his protests, but asked him to pick me up from my grandmother's home the next day for my return trip to the railway station. That satisfied him somewhat and he relented in his fearful protests, afraid that my gesture of leaving him would be interpreted as unsatisfactory service on his part by his employer.

Although I left the car and got down, I realized that I had actually no place to go to. Many of my relatives, near and distant, lived among the multitudes of the great city that lay sprawled in front of me but I had no clue where they lived or how they lived. Over the years of disuse, the blood relations, once close, had gradually floated away, and the void left behind was the only reminder of their prior existence. Nevertheless, I felt strangely at peace with myself.

The great marble edifice of Lord Curzon, created out of money donated by the rich people of India at the expense of the poor, rose in front of me. It was as much a memorial to the distant queen who never visited her most lucrative dominion as to the sycophancy of her viceroy and the kings and zamindars of India, who had owed their existence to her name and fame. But whatever may have been the purpose behind building it, the structure itself was grandly beautiful, white, smooth, and harmonious, although a futile effort. I walked slowly on the pavement along the boulevard that ran in front of the memorial. The surroundings were beautiful and at that time of year, when the heat had not turned ferocious yet, it was pleasant in the tree-lined, wide streets with green open spaces—the Maidan, lying directly in front. This was probably the most British part of the city, along with the nearby areas of Esplanade, New Market, and Park Street, names that by themselves evoked a not so distant but a very different past. The city and its citizens were in hurry, as was apparent from the rush of traffic all around me, and there was no time to think about the past. People were driving to their future, full of hope but also anxiety.

I had time in my hands as the work in Samir's shed had finished unexpectedly early and I just wandered along the streets without any purpose. Many thoughts crowded into my mind and flew away without forming themselves, without the benefit of clarity that comes with communication. I wanted to speak to someone, not anyone. We spend so much time with others, talking to them, laughing with them, but it is rare that one finds the right combination of time, space, person, and the state of mind when on one hand thoughts form and on the other they are communicated to an understanding and sympathetic ear. It is then one realizes what every man being on island may mean. Somehow, it occurred to me that Kajal could have been the person at that moment, with whom I could have attempted to make sense of the world of my thoughts. Although there was a lot of me that she didn't know yet, it felt that she would try to understand without being judgemental. Somehow I felt it would have been nice if Kajal had been with me on that leisurely day in Calcutta. But as soon as the thought appeared in my subconscious mind, I willed consciously to drive it away, conscious of both its utter impossibility and it not being 'right'. My innate sense of loyalty and morality led me to think about Riya, sitting somewhere miles away, in a world, utterly strange and unknown to me. But there was not much that I could think of.

I came back to my immediate surroundings of time and space as a curious-looking phaeton overtook me. It was being driven by a thin, bearded man, who was sitting atop, wearing a waist-coat over a white kurta pyjama, that had seen better days just like his vehicle, holding the reins of an ancient horse. It was a curious contraption in today's age of cars and buses, a throwback to the days when Calcutta, as also India whose capital it was, was being ruled by formally dressed, stiff, upper lipped, and fair-skinned Victorian Englishmen. I could almost imagine a Victorian lady, wearing her elaborate dress and coiffeur, totally unsuited to the tropical climate of the city, sitting upright in her carriage, thinking of her next port of social call, trying to keep herself amused in these exotic and unfamiliar surroundings, miles away from the wet, green fields of a Cotswold village, where she had grown up. Was she as happy, involved and excited in living in an exotic foreign place like Riya was or was she confused and uncomfortable away from her home?

Another hand-pulled rickshaw went past me—again a diminishing remnant of another era. A scrawny Bihari man, not long accustomed to the chaotic traffic of the megapolis, was desperately pulling a rather plump, fair, and bespectacled man who knew his place in his city, each separated from the other in a way that made the absence of a partition between them irrelevant. A newly-famous Bengali actress was giving an interview to a reporter of a TV channel, with Shaheed Minar, once called the Ochtorloney monument, in the background. A small spontaneous crowd had assembled around her, much to her satisfaction, and was gawking at the scene. The small TV crew was busy making sure that none of those unwanted crowd would inadvertently enter the camera frame. Watching the scene, I was transported in my mind to the simple-minded village women of Laldih and their untiring struggle for their and their families' lives, as I stared at the modern, liberalized India finding her feet, outside the camera frame, but no less real for being so.

Sometime later, walking alone absentmindedly, I reached Park Street, yet another attempt of the British to recreate something familiar. It had been something like their Oxford Street, back in London, in the heart of a city that they had created out of an unfamiliar and unknown land, one that they never grew their roots in, and inhabited by a people whom they never understood. The street was lined with restaurants with names like 'Mocambo' and 'Flurry's', once almost wholly owned, managed, and patronized by the British gentry of Calcutta, its officers, judges, traders, managers in foreign companies, and barristers, and their sociable wives. The names had stayed the same and so had some of the interiors and furniture. But the people, owners, managers, and clients, all had changed. An entirely new set of people—Indian businessmen, executives, tourists, and even families on an outing, now occupied the same seats. I wanted to have a meal at one of these famous restaurants of Park Street but somehow something inside me—perhaps hesitation, a sense of guilt that couldn't be articulated properly, unjustified extravagance, obligation to spend time with my grandmother—stopped me, and I found my feet taking me to a crowded corner that doubled up for a taxi stand. Another ancient, bulging black and yellow taxi drove me, down the spine of the city, past the streets of this once British city merging with the newly-created locales of the independent era, to my grandmother's house, where once my father had grown into a young man, years ago.

46

My grandmother was moving from room to room, holding a brass plate that had a burning mixture of incense, and some coconut fibres that were giving off a fragrant smoke. It was supposed to purify the home. This was a daily ritual that she had done every day since she had stepped into her married household, as a thirteen-year-old girl, ages ago. The ritual had not wavered even as her entire life and home had turned upside down when she, along with hundreds and thousands of other unsuspecting families, were forced to abandon their homes and world in Dhaka, today the capital of a separate country. They had moved to Calcutta during the cataclysmic events that followed the partition of India.

Evening had descended outside and it was getting dark. Electric lights were being switched on, one by one, in the neighbouring houses, visible through their open windows, giving glimpses of the lives of their inhabitants. A girl nearby was trying to practice music and the sound of her strained, high-pitched voice was wafting in through windows, past flimsy curtains bellowing in the wind.

'Would you go with me to the temple? I would also like to take you to meet Narikeldadu. Would you go?' my grandmother asked me, stopping briefly in front of me, offering me the brass plate whose smoke and warmth I was supposed to absorb in my palms, and then put them on my face as per the remnants of a custom that I had seen in my home since childhood. I knew that I might feel uncomfortable or bored, but I didn't want to disappoint my grandmother, who was also, to me, a life-like symbol of my father and his unspoken expectations.

'Okay, I am alright with it. Whenever you want,' I replied. She was visibly pleased. She had probably practised asking me that question a number of times, questioning herself about its appropriateness but now my answer had vindicated her faith. Soon she got ready, wearing the same saree, I noticed, that I had brought for her, that very morning. I realized if she was a symbol of my father to me, to her, I was also a symbol of the same person, her son. A son, she had brought up in the same house and whom she had seen go, years ago. Now his son had come back, even for only a couple of days.

We walked through narrow, brick paved lanes to my grandmother's temple. These lanes were lined with houses similar to ours, owned and occupied by families that had been forced to migrate in the aftermath of the partition, a couple of generations ago. But the present occupants had no time or inclination to remember and think about that other land, that other time, having come to terms with historic inevitability. Only occasionally, one would come across an old man with clouded, blinking eyes, staring into space, as if trying to unwrap himself from the cloak of past that just would not go.

'Do you remember your Dhaka days?' I asked my grandmother who had resumed her walk, after having stopped to greet some acquaintance in front of a titbit shop round the corner.

'How can one forget? That was our life, our world,' my grandmother replied after a brief pause. But neither did she say anything more nor did she seem inclined to elaborate any further. She had migrated with her brood of children and a disconsolate husband, with virtually nothing to carry to her new world. It had been a long, desperate struggle but my father and now I, in some way, stood for vindication of her struggles and faith in them. Now, she was going to her temple—the abode of her personal god—that had sustained her faith in those dark, hopeless days when it had almost been the only thing she had.

It was not a conventional temple but a memorial dedicated to a holy man, who had lived and died years ago, and whose legacy had been carried on, with some success, by his line of appointed successors and their dedicated group of disciples. Such holy men and their teachings had always been quite common in India, much before the invasion of twenty-four hour television channels, and the hordes of telegenic gurus and babas, who were later to be spawned as consequence. A dedicated group of followers, of all ages—but heavily skewed in favour of women—were sitting in a roughly circular ring, on the floor, around a large garlanded photograph of the original holy man, my grandmother's 'thakur'—literally, but not really, meaning god. I had seen a smaller version of the same photograph, mounted and garlanded, in my grandmother's bedroom, one of the few precious objects that she had managed to get with herself from Dhaka. Most of the devotees, some with their eyes closed with reverence, were swaying gently to the tune of a holy song—a 'kirtan,' that was being sung by person in saffron, accompanied by a sole harmonium. We sat quietly on the periphery of the circle, cross-legged, after having taken out our footwear, as is done before entering all Hindu temples.

There were a few, recently-constructed rooms, haphazardly located in the uneven courtyard surrounding the temple. Some acted as guestrooms, others as offices, one as a dispensary of medicines and one a library. Although no faith was aroused in my mind by the atmosphere but I was curious. My attitude to religion and god was uncertain and was yet unformed. I didn't have any strong views either way. Later, on our way to Narikeldadu, my grandmother told me that she considered herself blessed for having met her 'Thakur' and for having being initiated by him, when he was alive. That was in his original ashram, in the foothills of Chittagong, or 'Chattgram' as she called it long ago. She had visited him as a young mother, along with her husband and kids. One of those wide-eyed kids, for whom the long journey from Dhaka itself would have been an adventure, was my father, who was also nominally initiated by my enthusiastic grandmother. But that remote initiation had probably worn away over the years of western education and urban life and I hadn't seen my father profess or practice any faith in any institutionalized religion.

'Narikel' means coconut in Bengali and I don't know how or why Narikeldadu got his peculiar name. He had been my grandparents' friend, from their days of youth in Dhaka, and was more than a family member. The fact that I had only heard of him from my father but had never met him before was a reflection of the distance that had grown between me and my family. We walked up the narrow staircase of a non-descript building to Narikeldadu's room. There was no question of my grandmother informing him in advance of our coming to meet him. Fortunately, he was at home and promptly opened the blue wooden doors of his room.

'This is Bablu's son. I thought of bringing him to meet you,' my grandmother explained my presence while taking her seat on a large wooden box, covered with cloth, that doubled up as a bench. It was a single, not very small, but spartan room where Narikeldadu lived. I sat down on the single wooden chair with a straight back—one of the few objects in the room. Narikeldadu himself sat cross legged on his bed. A calendar, with a scene from Bhagvat Geeta being recited by Lord Krishna to Arjun, adorned one of the walls.

'Oh! He has grown up just like his father. I remember Bablu when he was this age. He came to offer me sweets on getting his first job, here in this same room,' Narikeldadu remarked, with a smile on his lips and a distant gaze in his eyes. I was silent. I didn't know what to say or how to react. I felt maybe I should have got some sweets too or should have touched the feet of the old man, seeking his blessings, when we had entered the room. But the thought had not struck me, and now it was too late. Nevertheless, I was curious about this man. There was something about his demeanour, posture, and gaze that attracted me.

Narikeldadu had never married and while in Dhaka, had got involved with 'Anushilan Samiti'—a revolutionary group that had aimed at procuring India's freedom from the British rule through, if necessary, violent means. For that, he had been arrested, convicted, and sent to the Cellular jails in the Andamans, called 'Kala Pani' and had been released after long years, only in 1947. Since independence and partition, Narikeldadu had lived in Calcutta. He and some of his old colleagues from the Anushilan Samiti days had built this building for old revolutionaries like him, who had nowhere else to go. Over the years, most of them had withered and died, and now Narikeldadu worked as a full-time care taker in a hostel of young students, all boys from relatively poorer families, in the building.

'So, you are also an engineer, like your father? You are working in Jamshedpur, isn't it? That is good. I am very pleased about you,' Narikeldadu addressed me genuinely. 'It is good that you took time to visit your grandmother. You should try to come more often,' he added. He didn't mean to preach and there was definitely no accusatory tone in his voice.

Although there was a full-fledged kitchen for the hostel boys running downstairs, Narikeldadu preferred to cook his own food in the adjoining kitchen. Despite our protests, he made some tea for all of us and offered some typical Bengali sweets of puffed rice balls and jaggery—'moa'—which he took out from an old glass jar of Horlicks.' Contrary to my expectations, Narikeldadu did not appear to be a disillusioned man and left to himself, didn't like to talk about his past. He had turned religious or spiritual, and was living the remaining years of his life like a hermit. He was not a recluse, but alone and content, surrounded by the swirling city and its noise, grime, and tension but still untouched by them, in his solitude.

47

Kajal and Mr Kulkarni had gone to Nasik, a town in the heartland of Maharashtra, to attend the marriage of some close relative, Kajal's first cousin, in fact. In India, marriages are, more often than not, big occasions for distant relatives, separated by years and miles, to come together, for extended relations to be revalidated, for brothers, sisters and cousins to meet, and introduce their children to each other. These are also occasions where other marriages are arranged, prospective daughters-in-law and sons-in-law are evaluated and their parents approached, mostly under the eager eyes of mothers and aunts.

Kajal had no mother and I suspected very much whether Mr Kulkarni was particularly adapt for such purposes. Also, being a widow, however young, seriously disadvantaged Kajal in such arranged marriage scenario. But most importantly I was sure Kajal was different and would make her own choices and decisions, ready to take responsibility for their consequences, as she had already taken once, so tragically.

Though I was friends with both Mr Kulkarni and Kajal, and should have liked the thought of Kajal re-marrying and settling down again, strangely, a part of me seemed not too pleased at this prospect of her moving away to live her own life, with some unknown figure at some unknown place.

Despite Kajal not being there, I still went to Laldih that Sunday. It was the first time I was travelling alone in our familiar bus as it bumped and strutted over uneven routes through empty scrublands and sparsely populated forests, passing small roadside hamlets and an occasional small town. Although I had taken exactly the same route and journey on many occasions in the past, it felt different that day and although a fellow passenger, a dark man, who almost continuously smoked thin beedis, occupied the window seat next to me, it appeared to be empty. I could easily have avoided taking the solitary trip to Laldih that weekend but somehow I needed to show, to myself, that Kajal was not the sole reason for my endless trips to the GSS villages, and that my work, my involvement with Nirmaladi's organization and the women of Laldih and other villages went beyond Kajal.

It was a sunny, clear day in early summer and although it was warm, it had not yet turned unbearably hot as it would, in a few days. Nirmaladi was at home and was, as always, visibly pleased at my arrival. If she was a bit disappointed at Kajal's absence, it didn't show. Nirmaladi, from the very first time when we had met, had reciprocated my tremendous respect for her, with an easy affection that was difficult to explain. It went far beyond an appreciation of whatever contribution I had made to the GSS work, precious little as it was. We were sitting in the verandah in front of her small house, on bamboo settees. The women of a neighbouring village had started making these recently, drawing on their ancient traditions, prodded and helped by Nirmaladi.

'The women are very excited about the packing machine that you have arranged for them. Some of them have become quite expert at handling it too. They are very happy, thanks to you,' Nirmaladi remarked, sipping tea from her stainless steel tumbler. She always made much of whatever I did. But Samir had been true to his word and as soon as I had confirmed to him on phone, after having discussed with Nirmaladi, he had sent his most trusted boy to the village. The boy had installed the machine, trained some of the women on the machine, collected the money, and returned.

'Yes. It would be easier to sell packaged food. Maybe, we can buy some printed labels too. Also, I think it is high time we apply for procuring a government certificate for food production. It helps in selling products, especially to companies with rigid and impersonal rules,' I replied, my mind racing to future milestones and goals, forgetting to sip the tea.

'Yes. All will happen in due time. Not that we didn't try it earlier but the procedure to get the certificate was just too difficult and distant. It takes time and money for simple villagers to go to Jamshedpur, again and again, to meet some clerk in some obscure office, who may or may not be there,' Nirmaladi said. Having undertaken the journey many times myself, I appreciated the truth in her statement that was probably lost to the clerk and his officer, who sat in their offices in Jamshedpur.

'By the way, Kajal was telling me the other day that you are waiting for your collegemate, Riya, to return from the USA so that you two can get married and settle down,' Nirmaladi said, changing the subject from the immediate concerns of GSS to my distant prospects of life. It was the first time we were talking about Riya. It was also the first time, I realized, that we were talking in Kajal's absence.

'Yes. At least that is what the plan looks like,' I replied. I tried to sound confident although the conviction in my heart was not as strong as I would have liked.

'That's nice,' Nirmaladi replied. After a brief pause she added, 'I have never met Riya and I know precious little about her. But is she eager and waiting to return? There are people like that. I had a few Indian students when I was teaching in the USA, who were determined to return to India as soon as possible. I don't know whether they did.'

It was a question that demanded a straight-forward and honest answer. It was also a question that I had been avoiding, for quite some time. We were both silent and probably my silence told Nirmaladi more than what I could possibly have articulated in words.

'Because if she brings herself to come back to be with you, it is still possible that she would turn out to be happy and your mutual love may make everything else immaterial eventually. But it is better to be open-minded about this and not be trapped into a decision that you took once upon a time,' Nirmaladi said with wisdom and obvious concern.

'Has she not asked you ever to join her in the USA? I am sure you were a very good student in college,' Nirmaladi asked after a while. With anybody else, I might have felt uncomfortable facing so many questions about my life in such a short time but nobody had ever tried. I didn't feel uncomfortable. Instead, I felt glad that I was talking with Nirmaladi about things and issues that I had not been able to face myself. She was not thinking for me, she was only helping me to think, and there lies a tremendous difference between the two.

'Yes. She did try a number of times to convince me to go to the USA and study there. Even her parents did. But lately she stopped, maybe out of hopelessness. She herself appears to be quite happy and involved there. She would probably apply for PhD in her University there,' I replied, eventually.

'I am sure you do understand that I am your friend, although far older than you, and that I am speaking to you, at this moment, purely out of the spirit of friendship. I know that every individual is different and what is true for one is not necessarily true for another. But you know sometimes it helps to talk to somebody, to look at things more clearly. Left to ourselves, we sometimes miss out on some obvious things as we become used to one particular view. This has happened with me many a times. Not that I can claim that I have myself made all the right decisions, all the time. Looking into one's own heart and mind is much more difficult than looking out into the world,' Nirmaladi said, looking out from the verandah.

A few yellow flowers had come up in the flower bed, laboriously created out of rough soil. In a few days, they would vanish as the sun would beat down everything to dry earth except the gulmohurs and amaltashes that thrived on the branches of tall trees, even at the height of summer.

48

Gautam had cleared the main tests of the three-stage examination that allows one to enter the premium civil services of India. These mains are considered the toughest of the three and clearing them was a big step towards his eventual goal of becoming an IAS officer. Now only the interview remained for which he would be going to Delhi very soon. He was naturally happy but not elated. There was precious little that he could do to prepare himself for the interview, and the subjectivity and uncertainty of the exercise bothered him a little.

'Pankaj, can you help me by conducting a few mock interviews? You will ask me questions as if you were an interviewer and I would answer. It would help me a lot,' Gautam asked me one evening.

Although I was probably the closest to him in the hostel, still the fact that he considered me, of all people, for this task gladdened me. Kajal and Mr Kulkarni had not yet returned from Maharashtra, and I had been feeling empty and at loose ends to an unexpected extent. They had decided to take a detour to the village of Shirdi, and pray at the famous temple there.

'Anytime. Anywhere. Although, I don't know whether I will be able to stand up to the task. The interviewers for your interview would be far more learned and evolved people, I am sure,' I replied.

'That might be true. But it is really a matter of getting used to the idea of thinking and answering logically and clearly. Besides you are sufficiently well-read and knowledgeable yourself. It's a pity that you never thought of attempting to appear for the exams,' Gautam replied.

Just like Riya, Gautam had tried many a time to enthuse me to the idea of appearing in the civil services exams, and just like her, had failed. But the reasons were different. In case of Riya, it was my utter lack of inclination and even a positive disinclination to leave my country and settle abroad that stopped me, whereas in Gautam's case, it was my lack of ambition and confidence that had stopped me from attempting to live the life that I believed to be noble but well beyond me.

'What about you? Do you think you would continue in this job? Would you be happy doing what you are doing, all your life?' Gautam asked me. We were sitting in my room. My roommate was on shift duty. It was late evening and we were waiting for dinner when we would go down to the dining room of the hostel.

'I don't know. Everything appears to be uncertain and in a flux. My job is okay, although I am more satisfied and happy about my involvement and activities with the GSS work. But then I can't support myself and my family, working fulltime with GSS,' I replied. I realized, even while answering, that Riya and her plans were also a big factor in my thinking about my future and in my inability to come to terms with it.

'I hope to get to do things that we love doing, and

which will remain meaningful and useful too,' Gautam said with a sigh. 'I see so many people who are living one life while wanting to live another. I hope we don't end up doing that,' he said. He was in an expansive and yet profound frame of mind.

'You know, maybe, I would accompany you to Delhi when you go there for your interview. That way I can show you around Delhi. Riya had written in her last letter that she would be coming to India around that time, so it suits me perfectly. Where would you be putting up? Have you thought of anything?' I asked Gautam. The idea just struck me and it appeared to be attractive. Maybe, within a few months, Gautam will embark on a different life path, separate from me, forever.

'Yes. I would love that. That would really be good. But I haven't yet thought about where to stay. I have never visited Delhi. I was thinking of living in some budget hotel, somewhere near the railway station but you being there at the same time, would really help me,' Gautam said, visibly pleased with my idea. 'Let's book our tickets together as I already have my interview dates. Would you travel second class?' Gautam enquired.

'Yes. I always travel second class. Let us book our tickets tomorrow itself. Sometimes it gets difficult to get reservations, especially during these summer vacations,' I replied. Although I could actually afford travelling in air-conditioned coaches as the second-class coaches sometimes became very hot in summers, still something in me, my upbringing, had always stopped me from paying for tickets of those coaches.

'So it is settled then. Let's go for dinner. It is almost

nine. From tomorrow we can start our mock interviews before dinner,' Gautam said, looking at his HMT wrist watch. There was no need for him to thank me in so many words. I knew that he felt like thanking me, but it was an act of unnecessary politeness bordering on formality between friends.

'Let's go. I hope they don't serve bitter gourds again,' I replied, laughing. Both of us hated bitter gourds. Actually, I never knew anybody in my hostel who liked them but still they appeared in our dinner table, day after day, or so it seemed.

49

Surprisingly, our postman used to deliver letters separately to each of our hundred odd rooms in the hostel, instead of dumping them all together in the ground floor. We didn't make much of it then, taking it for granted. I don't think even the old man made much of it, accepting his labour as his routine job, just like getting his Diwali and Holi tips from each of us. He used to slip our letters beneath our closed doors, through the narrow gap between them and the floor. We would, more often than not, be away in the factory during his daily visits, sometime in the afternoon. Often we would feel the letters at our feet when we entered our rooms, prompting us—on reflex—to touch our forehead as a mark of asking forgiveness from the goddess of learning, for having touched paper—the sign of learning—with feet, which was a sign of disrespect. It was one of those many things which every person grows up doing (since his childhood) as a part of his culture that become a part of him.

It had been quite some days since I had received any letter from anywhere. On that Tuesday, as I entered my hostel room, there were three letters at one go, pushed through the gap, awaiting me. One was clearly from Riya, with its overseas postal envelope and USA stampings that

I had come to recognize. The second was a familiar sky blue inland letter of postal department with my name and address written neatly in my father's sure handwriting, emphasizing each letter and word. But it was the third letter that really caught my attention. I was not expecting any letter from Kajal, and there never had been any earlier occasion for her to write to me as she had never left Jamshedpur since the first time we had met. Further, she and Mr Kulkarni had gone for barely a ten days' visit to Maharashtra. Nevertheless, inexplicable and unexpected as it was, I was joyous as well as satisfied in a curious way.

After depositing my helmet in its usual resting place and taking my shoes off, it was my father's letter that I tore open first. Although, it was an inland letter, the sky blue paper inside had been shared by my father, mother and sister, each writing a short letter, overlapping others' in content and spirit. The letters were on simple, expected lines, reassuring and revalidating relations and worlds that tried to, unconsciously, create an illusion of unchanging permanence. They talked of mundane lives and events, assuring of their well-being, enquiring about mine, as they had always done. It was a letter from a port to a ship.

Riya's envelope was lightest in weight but heaviest in import. She was almost sure to get an offer for doing her PhD in her own University and was unabashedly elated about it. She had apparently improved tremendously as a student since going to the USA and felt appreciated as one, which she readily reciprocated. One of her professors had helped her professionally and influenced her to do her PhD and she was glad. Although she briefly wrote about the topic of her proposed PhD thesis, it was too obscure and distant for me to understand. The real import of her narrative for me was that she had decided, on her own, to stay in the USA for a considerably longer period of time, with no certainty even thereafter. I was not sure what Riya expected me to do or whether she indeed expected anything of me. In her letter, she barely touched up on our relationship, its future prospects, and the impact of her decision on our future. The news should have shocked me but maybe due to the matter of fact tenor of her letter, or maybe deep inside me I was half expecting such a turn of events, it didn't really shock me as it should have. Rather it appeared as a confirmation of a truth that we both suspected had already been there, somewhere hidden beneath.

I had kept Kajal's letter for the last. It was totally unexpected and maybe because of that, brought sudden joy as well. Although she was completely involved in the various marriage ceremonies at her relatives' place, she had found herself a bit of time alone, even amidst the crowd. Apparently, it was this feeling of being out of place that prompted her to write to me. I wondered 'Why me?' Had she wondered the same too?

She wrote that she did think about me and our weekend trips together in the ramshackle bus to Laldih and other GSS villages. Though in a way she was enjoying all the marriage ceremonies surrounding her, mostly because of their novelty, she was glad that she was soon going to return to her own city, own place under the sun, routine of life, and to do things that mattered to her. It was clear from her letter that she was at peace with herself and her place in life, and that she felt she belonged to her place. Such complete contentment had always eluded me and whereas Jamshedpur didn't seem be my place, Delhi, the city where I had grown up, had also lost her hold over me, if ever there was one.

I was drifting between two places, two lives, probably looking for something else. But even then I realized that it was not the places themselves but how I looked at them that made all the difference. In many ways, Kajal's letter was the most intimate of the three, without any sense of need for dutifulness, a person writing to another, sharing her mind and heart, without any self-consciousness. It was like a part of her. I folded the letters slowly and kept them carefully. Riya's letter went to the bundle of her letters that I had kept stored, from her first to this one. I had to find a place to keep Kajal's letter, her first.

50

Kajal's narration of their trip to Maharashtra shocked me, to say the least. It had not only been an innocent detour to Shirdi that had delayed Mr Kulkarni and Kajal, as she recounted. We were, once again, sitting in their drawing room.

'My dear father, despite himself, very nearly managed to marry me off for a second time. We have known Makrand and his family for years. They are, in fact, distantly related to us from my mother's side. Despite everything, Makrand wants to marry me and his parents too would like the match,' said Kajal. By 'everything' Kajal meant her first marriage and its tragic end. Murthy's death never went comfortably far away. 'They were so eager that it was suggested that we extend our trip and the marriage be ceremonized at Shirdi,' Kajal recounted. It had turned up all so suddenly, just after she had posted her letter to me.

I was too shocked to react or to say anything at the prospect of Kajal's sudden marriage. But I was shocked at my reaction too. After all, it was perfectly natural and even desirable, from all accounts, for Kajal to remarry and from what she had briefly told me that there was nothing remotely objectionable in what had unfolded or in the proposal that had come to her. If anything, the proposal was eminently suitable, but somehow its suitability irritated me. I kept quiet with questioning eyes, urging Kajal to complete her story.

'It was only Papa, at the end, who put his foot down. Although he is naturally eager to get me married, but perhaps he sensed that I was not totally comfortable, especially at the pace at which the entire thing was unfolding. So it has been delayed with an informal understanding that if everything remains as they are, maybe they will go ahead,' Kajal said. She used the word 'they' instead of 'we' as if she was talking about somebody else.

'What do you think or feel? What is your reaction?' I managed to barely whisper, still too shocked at the unexpected revelation that had hit me like a sledgehammer.

'I am yet to make up my mind,' Kajal replied after some thought. 'On one hand, I really don't want to leave Jamshedpur, the work, and my involvement with Nirmaladi and GSS is very important to me. But I can sense that Papa would be secretly relieved to see me married and settled down. I can't really blame him, looking at the kind of society and age that we live in,' she added. Nobody could blame Mr Kulkarni. On the contrary, he had always given every latitude and opportunity to Kajal to decide her course of life. It was strange that Makrand had not entered the discussion.

'What does Mr Makrand do? Where does he live?' I asked Kajal, adding a conscious respectability to the name that I had heard barely a few minutes ago, for the first time.

'Makrand lives and teaches in London. He was a student in humanities—sociology or anthropology or something like that, he told me. I have known him only very little, over the years, mostly on similar family occasions. But it seems that he fancies me, and despite knowing about my previous marriage, wants to marry me. In fact, he told me that he always wanted to marry me but had never expressed it before,' Kajal replied, inadvertently avoiding eye contact with me.

'At least, it is good to know that someone still fancies you. It is an ego booster,' Kajal said, smiling. 'Maybe, it is really better to marry someone who fancies you than to marry a person whom you like,' she added, this time looking straight at me.

It appeared to me as if Kajal had more or less reconciled herself to the direction in which destiny was, so unexpectedly, prodding her. Despite whatever we may assume, our lives are more often a result of events and our reaction to them rather than a grand strategy that we think for ourselves. We don't live our lives, it is the other way around.

'Do you love Mr Makrand? What is his surname, by the way?' I asked Kajal, almost challenging her, for some unknown reason. What was there to challenge and who was I, anyway, to throw any challenge at her?

'No, I have no delusions about that. It also probably depends upon how we define love. I like him. He is a nice, warm person, and a thorough gentleman. I don't feel anything about him as I once felt for Murthy. But one can't be lucky twice, right? That would be like being too greedy, isn't it?' Kajal answered, throwing a question back at me, but she didn't seem to expect any answer. She already knew what she wanted to believe.

'Yes, at least two men have loved you, unconditionally. Even that is rare in today's world,' I said. I still felt uncomfortable and a sort of knot was forming in the pit of my stomach.

'That's true for you also. We are all very lucky, are we not?' Kajal said with a long sigh, raising herself from the chair. 'But life is more than love and all that. One needs to have peace at home and an understanding partner who allows and helps you to flourish, develop yourself, do your own thing, and who respects you. A person whom you love may not be the person who does all that,' she added.

'What about love? How can you live your entire life with a person whom you don't love?' I queried. There was a sudden edge in my voice that I recognized with surprise.

'It again depends upon what one understands by love. If I may, you make too much out of your own concept of love. Love happens but it also grows and fades. As for me, love should embrace and pervade our lives. Life should not chase love. But everybody has to find his or her answers, I guess,' Kajal replied, looking at my eyes, trying to understand and make me understand too.

'You seem to have worked out everything, is it? It seems you have done an entire PhD on love and life?' I countered, with a touch of inexplicable sarcasm in my voice.

'Yes. I had a lot of time to think about such things. After Murthy, I didn't feel like talking to or meeting people. It was so sudden. My entire life, as it was poised to be, vanished away in an instant, just like that. I had to learn to make sense of my life, to get back my bearings,' Kajal replied with neither bitterness nor self-pity in her voice. I felt ashamed at myself, for my pettiness. It was me who needed to think, perhaps.

That night, I had my dinner at Kajal and Mr Kulkarni's home. Although, the food was, as usual, nice and sumptuous without being flashy and formal, my mind was not much in it. It seemed to me that Kajal was already beginning to drift away and that Mr Kulkarni was remote. I noticed however that Mr Kulkarni never once broached the subject of Kajal and Makrand in front of me, as if nothing unusual had happened during their Maharashtra trip. Maybe, he just didn't want to publicize anything before things were finalized, or he didn't want to pressurize Kajal into any decision. But I imagined myself outside the invisible but strict domains of an age old family with high walls barring my way. It was a new feeling for me, at their home. We talked about Shirdi, Sai baba, Jamshedpur's weather, and about many things that were discovered to fill up an empty space that engulfed us. It felt awkward, my mind drifting to what Kajal had told me that evening.

I returned to my empty hostel room, later in the night. My former roommate, Rajesh, had gone off to his hometown to finalize his own engagement ceremony with his college principal's daughter, a girl whom he had always liked but never gathered enough courage to say so. However, his parents had come to know of his wish, and as the girl's family belonged to the same caste, were respectable and willing, they had 'arranged' the marriage, rather swiftly. Though he had insisted, I had managed to extricate myself from attending the engagement ceremony by promising that I would definitely go to his ancestral village for the marriage ceremony that was supposed to take place later in winter. These crowded ceremonies among strangers always bored me. However, on that night, I felt Rajesh was lucky to have such a simple, straight-forward and uncomplicated life. He seemed to be living from day to day, certain of his present, not overtly worried about his future. One values that most which is missing in one's own life.

51

I always loved travelling by trains, even when the journeys were undertaken in hot, non-air conditioned carriages, during the peak of Indian summers. While growing up, travelling by plane never came to our minds. Only the very rich or people like my father, whose official trips were sponsored by their employers, travelled by plane. Besides, Jamshedpur didn't have a commercial airport. But this time, I was not undertaking the long journey to Delhi alone, as was usual. Gautam was travelling and sharing the second-class carriage with me, and another family whose father figure was also working in our company, as we soon found out. Those long journeys provided me with a sense of solitude, a state of mental stupor, and a physical break from everyday realities of world in a way that fascinated me. It was not so much the eagerness to reach my destination but the journey itself, especially during the day time, when the entire age-old Indian panorama unfolded in front of my eyes, through the open windows, with its sights, sounds, and smells that kept me enthralled in my solitary hours. But it was different that time. With Gautam, the inevitable conversations, touching upon topics of common interests, began to flow soon after we left Jamshedpur station. Gautam was clear in his mind. He was going to give his best go at the interview, as he had done in the written exams. But if he was not able to get into the IAS that year, he would again try next year with much more preparation. I liked his single-mindedness, self-belief, confidence but most of all, I liked the clarity of his mind about what he wanted to do, at least at that point in his life.

We conducted a couple of mock interviews, but the journey was too long to be consumed only by those. By the time we reached Dehri-on-Sone, our conversation had taken up a life of its own. In those days, nobody thought of objecting to anyone smoking in a public place and soon Gautam had lit up one of his trademark Wills Navy Cut, taking care to blow the smoke out of the open window. The family we shared the carriage with, didn't seem to mind or even if they did, it didn't show.

Soon, I found myself sharing my thoughts about Riya's latest letter telling me of her decision to pursue a PhD in the USA, about Kajal's prospects of getting married, my work with GSS and the villagers, and what I wanted to do with my life. I had not wanted to talk on these topics, but somehow the tension in my stomach prompted me on as the scenes of the red soiled villages changed in a series of postcard-like photographs outside my window. It was a slow train and was stopping at many small stations and even sometimes, in the middle of nowhere, for no apparent reason. But I didn't mind.

'Look, I don't think you should stay committed to Riya, especially after this letter. That is stopping you from thinking clearly about your own future and what you want to do with it. I really don't see her coming back and living in India, forget Jamshedpur, from what you have told me,' said Gautam, after a few minutes of hearing my intermittent ramblings. He had neither doubted his conclusions, nor hesitated in articulating, or giving his unambiguous recommendations about somebody else's life, my life.

'But I love her and I think she does too. We have given our words to each other to get married,' I protested, testing Gautam's theory with my own. Besides, I had announced my pious intentions to my parents and her.

'I believe you do love her and maybe she does too. But love is not the only thing in life. And love grows and fades, it appears and vanishes. Also, all feelings of love may not translate into sharing lives, or committing to life-long attachment. Besides, it is not going anywhere, as I see it,' he said. He had hardly ever before talked about me and Riya, although he had known about her and yet that day something had prompted him to talk so openly and frankly about my relationship. Maybe, he felt that he would, sooner than later, leave me and Jamshedpur to pursue his life elsewhere, and would never again get a chance to share his opinions about my life. Maybe, he felt obliged to share his views as a friend, hoping that such would help me think and decide what I wanted. Maybe, it was just the long, hot journey.

'And I also think she is taking you for granted. She can't expect you to wait forever, with an uncertain future. I think it is time for you to talk directly to her about her plans. You told me she is going to be in Delhi this time. Why don't you talk to her, know her mind, and come to some conclusions to resolve your future?' he asked.

We had stepped down on to an almost deserted railway platform. The train had stopped on a small station with a solitary station master's office, a never-heard-before name was written in yellow and black signage as they do in every railway station in India, and there was precious little else. There was a gulmohur tree in full bloom in the station courtyard, rearing its head with electric hues of red, unnoticed by the passengers. A few others had also got down from the train and were stretching their limbs or looking at the signal, waiting for it to turn green.

'Yes. I think this time I am going to sit and talk to Riya about what she wants to do and how she sees our lives unfolding from that. I also have to see what I want to do with my life, otherwise. I wish I was as clear about my life as you are about yours,' I told Gautam.

'Maybe, the question of your relationship with Riya is linked with what you want to do with your life. Perhaps, the resolution of the first would automatically resolve the second,' Gautam answered. 'None of us really know, for sure, how our lives would unfold, but still one can't really keep drifting. For example, Kajal never thought that Murthy would die so suddenly and so tragically in the train accident, but she is carrying on with other things, changing her course and life, according to events as they unfold. I really quite admire her for that,' he said.

This was the first that Gautam had spoken about Kajal that morning. He had known Kajal, on and off, mainly through me and quite clearly admired and respected her.

'You know, that train accident must have happened somewhere very near to this place. It was the same train and the same route,' he said.

The thought suddenly struck me and I felt a shiver running down my spine. It was almost a real physical sensation.

'Yes. So many families and so many lives must have changed forever in the split of a second. Life is really so uncertain and despite our best laid plans, throws up things at us which we can never imagine,' Gautam replied. He had turned almost philosophical, without any effort or pretence.

'By the way, don't you think Kajal likes you? I think she does, even if she may not have admitted it to herself, knowing the futility of the situation and also about your feelings for Riya,' Gautam added after a few silent, heavy moments.

It was a subject, one of Kajal's feelings for me or the other way round, that had never come up for discussion ever earlier. It was a subject that I had never even allowed to enter the realms of my conscious thoughts, even in moments of my most precious solitude.

'Do you really think so?' I asked, wanting to hear again the confirmation of an opinion that he had already articulated quite clearly.

'I am quite sure about it. But she does not want to encourage her thoughts as she does not know what you feel or think about her, or about yourself and your life. I can understand her more clearly than I can understand your mind and heart,' Gautam replied.

The signal had turned green and a guard in black coat was waving a green flag from the last carriage in the rear of the long, snake-like train, to the accompaniment of the long-drawn sound of a whistle, signalling to the absent-minded, that the train was about to resume its long journey. The uncertainty of the stop had given way to the certainty of journey.

52

Gautam had promised to come home for lunch next Sunday, the day after his interview. It was decided that I would come and fetch him from his Paharganj hotel where he had checked in. I had accompanied him in his search for a clean, decent hotel, close to the railway station, where we had disembarked after a journey that had eventually lasted for more than thirty hours—two more than scheduled. Although, I had not consulted my parents before inviting Gautam, I was reasonably sure that he would be more than welcome in our house, not only because he was my friend but because of his innate charm and what he himself was.

But before that, I was to meet Riya, who was already in Delhi, having reached a couple of days earlier. As I reached home late at night, having crossed the face of Delhi that was increasingly appearing to be unfamiliar, through the streets of India's proud diplomatic enclaves, I thought it prudent to wait for the night and ring up Riya next morning. We, in our home, had recently acquired a telephone after waiting for years. Life had become vastly more comfortable for my parents, whose only son was living hundreds of kilometres away, and whose daughter had begun to go to a college. I didn't want to appear too eager to meet Riya. Though I was keen on seeing her, this time the nature of my eagerness was different. It was not about seeing her as I used to, to resume talking to her, but to clear up the misty clouds that had lately developed between us. In a way, I was keen to see her as she saw herself, not as I imagined her to be.

But despite my eagerness, I was not much disappointed the next morning at the knowledge that Riya had left very early to go to Surajkund, in the outskirts of Delhi. Surajkund, those days was the place where people of Delhi went to consume cheap booze and it was only recently that it had begun to gain an incipient reputation as a place of an annual crafts and cultural jamboree. Riya's mother was, surprisingly for a weekday, at home. It was she who picked up the phone.

'No, she is not at home. She left early in the morning for Surajkund fair. No I don't know when she would be back,' she said. Her voice was always cool but that morning there was no small polite talk, as was her wont, between us. Riya had known about my arrival so it was a bit unexpected that she had left so early and that too for Surajkund.

'Yes. I would tell her that you had called up or you can try late in the evening. By the way, Riya has come this time with her academic supervisor and she would, I guess, be busy showing him the sights of Delhi, as this is his first visit to India. She might have told you already,' Mrs Malhotra replied to my request about Riya's whereabouts. She had not asked for our phone number. It was doubly strange that Riya had not mentioned about her supervisor's trip in her last letter. Maybe, I thought, his trip had been decided at the last moment, and there had been no time to inform me. If I was looking for any signs of Riya wanting to return to India, I was definitely not getting any.

The entire day loomed empty in front of me. That day, sitting in my room, cooled by the moist air thrown by the noisy blades of our giant cooler, surrounded by the familiar objects of my home where I had grown up, I decided that it was time for me to ask Riya whether she intended to come back to India at all ever, and how she looked at our future together. I wanted to give her an opportunity to clear her mind of obligations and commitments that may have been, given at a different time and when we were different or at least she was, very substantially. I wanted a decision to be taken, a resolution to be made but I wanted Riya to make the decision and resolve the situation. But unlike earlier times, I was prepared to face and accept everything and hopefully get on with it. I wanted to give her a way out. I wanted to give myself a way out without the guilt—but of course, I didn't realize it then.

Later in the evening, I found Riya back in her home when I rang up again. This time, she picked up the phone herself.

'Hello. I was waiting for you to return. Let's meet up tomorrow for lunch. At our old Asiad village place. Is it ok with you? I heard that your supervisor is here too. How was Surajkund, by the way?' I asked.

I thought there was more than a moment of silence before Riya answered. 'It was nice. Steve loved the work of the rural artisans and the performing artists. Yes, we can meet but Steve will be there, I guess. I can't leave him all alone as it was on my insistence that he has come all the way. It is his first visit to India and he is totally unfamiliar with the place, as you can imagine,' she said.

This surely was a big surprise for me and although I had

no idea about Riya's supervisor, I felt him to be encroaching on areas where he had no business to be. But I had to talk to Riya and appear unconcerned too.

'Of course, naturally. But then let's meet for coffee and then maybe we can both go and pick him up for lunch, from wherever he is living. If that suits you,' I wanted some time alone with Riya, and this was a way out without appearing to be prickly.

'Okay. That's fine. Let's meet at Nirula's in Chanakyapuri. See you tomorrow then. I am feeling a bit tired. It has really been a long day. Goodnight,' Riya replied, stifling a yawn and I could hear the distinct sound of the receiver being kept down.

The cloud had frozen into ice and was weighing down inside my chest. Love didn't seem to have anything to do with it. That night, I wished I could talk to Kajal, or even to Gautam but I was alone, or at least, I felt alone, in my own home.

53

It was still early in the morning and I was among the very first customers at Nirula's. Soon it would fill up with the hordes of insatiable youth of new India to an extent that people would be irritatingly standing behind chairs, waiting for the customer sitting on it, to finish with whatever he might be having. But so early in the morning, it was still calm and peaceful, as if preparing for the deluge to come.

Soon, I saw Riya enter through the glass doors of the restaurant. She was wearing an ankle-length, black and white polka dotted skirt and a matching black cotton top with a wide leather belt. Her hair, I noticed, had undergone yet another transformation and was crinkled and 'permed'. She appeared to be in the best of health. I could positively see a tinge of glow in her face. But as she took her chair opposite me with a slight familiar smile, I realized that Riya was, that morning, not her usual spontaneous, effusive self. She appeared relaxed but reclusive, a bit absent-minded, and a little distant. She started the conversation after we had ordered something at the counter.

'Look. It is good that we have met. I want to discuss something with you. I wanted to do this earlier, but I didn't want to write a letter as I would not have been able to explain properly,' Riya said. Her initial uncertainty had evaporated and Riya was bringing herself deliberately on a course that appeared to have been rehearsed many times earlier, in solitude. It seemed that she had thought about our meeting beforehand and had something on her mind. I waited, looking into her eyes. Although I had wanted to, I had, till that time, said nothing.

'You know that I beseeched you innumerable times to move to the USA, and only you know for whatever reasons you refused to go,' she said. I knew that already, of course. 'Please, don't get me wrong, please. In spite of the fact that we loved each other, and in a way, still do, I can't delude you or myself, with an unfounded belief that I would return to India, on some uncertain distant future date. I think my life and work are set there and I am not ready, at least at this stage of my life, to exchange that for whatever India can offer. Let us accept the inevitable and stop hanging onto something that has no future,' she said.

The words that came out of her lips were too structured, too accurate to have been spontaneous. She had clearly given a lot of thought to this conversation. By a strange quirk of coincidence or telepathy, she had pre-empted me and broached the difficult subject that I had thought of and by doing so, had spared me.

'I may or may not ever feel the same way for anybody as I felt for you. But there is more to life than love and feelings, as important as they are. It would probably had been different had you decided to move to the USA when I asked you to, but that was then,' she added. There was a faint hopelessness and an accusation that lined Riya's voice. She was looking down at the empty table top. Nirula's was slowly filling up as the time of the matinee show approached. We had forgotten to order anything from the self-service counters. There was a pregnant silence looming between us. Apparently, Riya had spoken as much as she had decided to and had nothing left to say. I felt as if she had spoken for both of us and there was nothing for me to add either. The operation was complete, swift and seemingly painless, at least, at that moment.

I knew that the moment demanded me to respond to what had just been said, but I couldn't bring myself to say anything. What could I have said? We both sat, tight-lipped, looking at every thing but at each other.

'Don't you have anything to say?' Riya asked me after some time. Her eyes told me that she wanted me to share some of the burden and the guilt.

'So this is it, is it? Maybe, you are right. We have moved on to different orbits over the years. I don't blame you or myself. Maybe it could have been different but it is not. I accept your decision, of course. It would be a change but I hope it would be eventually for better,' I said. The words automatically came out of me as if somebody else was speaking and I could observe them from far.

It was the first time in that morning that a small smile lit up Riya's face. Maybe it was my acceptance of her decision that relieved her, although both of us knew that I had no choice but to accept. But I was wrong, once again. She was smiling at her supervisor, who had just entered the restaurant. Steve had objected to us taking the trouble to pick him up from his hotel and had volunteered to find out Nirula's himself, with the aid of taxi drivers. Clearly, he had been successful.

Despite having aniticipated it, the very first thing that I

noticed about Steve, or rather couldn't help noticing, was that he was white. Everything else about his identity was secondary and even if I didn't want to accept it, the colour of his skin defined him, for me, at least till the time one comes to know better. But of course, I had neither the time nor the inclination to really know Steve better, as I realized that it would probably be my first and last interaction with Riya's supervisor. Suddenly, the thought struck me whether it would be my last meeting with Riya as well. I wanted to ask her but Steve was already with us and the conversation had turned to banal introductions, the heat of India, what was to be ordered, and how India was so very different from the USA.

As it turned out, it was indeed my last meeting with Riya. But as long as we both live, nothing is final about that. Maybe, someday, in some airport terminal, I may bump into her.

54

Although I had thought of preponing my journey back to Jamshedpur and accompanying Gautam the very next Monday, it seemed as an act of unnecessary cruelty on my family, especially on my mother, who had planned and anticipated my visit since the time I had written to her about it. I kept to myself what had transpired between me and Riya that morning at Nirula's. I didn't want to conceal it anymore than I wanted to elaborate upon it with my family. Besides, I was sure, soon my actions or rather the lack of them, would make it clear to them that things had changed. I didn't hazard any guesses on their reactions, but I was sure that theirs would be based on their concern for me and my happiness. As far as my reaction was concerned, I didn't feel particularly shattered or even self-pitingly sorrowful. I just felt empty as if a part of me had been uprooted from somewhere inside my chest. If my parents, my sister, or even Gautam, when he came for lunch next Sunday, detected any change in me, they didn't comment. Lunch was filled with usual small, polite talks, with Gautam profusely and sincerely praising my mother's cooking, much to her visible delight. His interview had gone well but it was difficult to guess what those grey men and women thought behind their thick glasses. I hoped Gautam had kept his radicalism under wraps as I had advised him to. That week in Delhi was the shortest of weeks. It was also in a way the longest of weeks. I just stayed at home, thinking about my life and possible future. But one cannot bring oneself to think like that. I just idled away, to the great joy of my mother who was getting the rare occasion of seeing her son at home, after so many years. And if questions arose in her mind about why I was not going out to meet Riya, as I usually did during my stays in Delhi, she didn't ask. My parents must have talked among themselves about the change that was apparent in me and must have been concerned but they kept their counsel, waiting from afar, watching to detect any sign that would tell them the story. But they didn't ask anything. Maybe, they knew me better than I knew myself.

That day was very hot and the summer sun had beaten down mercilessly all day on the dry earth and turned the city even more listless. I spent the entire day, cocooned in the moist air-laden, cooled room of my home but by the evening I was feeling a bit cramped and suffocated in the small, closed space, and longed for a whiff of fresh air. Fortunately, by that time, the sun had tired itself out and there was even a very slight tinge of coolness in the breeze, as if an unseasonal rain had fallen somewhere near. That was enough for me and I took off for the nearby Deer Park, as I remembered I used to do in my childhood. The park stood closest to wild nature that one could find in the heart of South Delhi. In that evening twilight, sitting on an earthen hillock, looking at the dusty plane, and jungle spread below me, where some day the battlements of the Sultans of Delhi must have feared the raids of marauding

Mongols, I felt my mind clearing itself. Some moments come, ever so rarely, in the lives of everyone and in societies too, that change the order of things. I felt at peace with the expanse of nature in front of me and was reminded of the red soil and the fields of Laldih. The memory of another twilight that I had spent there with Kajal floated into my empty mind. Vandana's smile, the chaos of the eager school children under her charge, the village women's anticipation for a hopeful future for their children, the calm and affectionate serenity of Nirmaladi, all beckoned me. I felt that somehow I belonged there, although I had barely known them for a year or so, far away from the familiar world wherein I had grown up. I was no longer ready to live somebody else's life, trapped by others' expectations. I wanted to live my life, do my things; and maybe I had inadvertently stumbled on my thing, but had lacked the courage to accept it. There was nothing that stopped me from doing what I wanted to do. There was no need for me to leave my job straight away, but I still could embrace my work and my involvement with Nirmaladi wholeheartedly, without the promise of another life, another future lurking somewhere in the dark recesses of my mind. I imagined how pleased and happy would Nirmaladi be with my new found intention. I imagined even Kajal would be happy. But most of all, I imagined I would be happy and at peace with myself, with my present.

I wanted to share my thoughts with someone, but I had only the slowly darkening wilderness around me to which flocks of dark birds were returning. I sat there, in that twilight in Delhi, looking at the sky changing colours from pink to purple to an inky blue-black, before I trekked back to my home, family, and life.

55

Later I realized that at almost the same time when Riya was pronouncing her terminal judgement on our future the morning at Nirula's in Delhi, Kajal was writing to Makrand. She did appreciate him for wanting to share his life with her and admitted that she had considered it seriously. Of course, she didn't divulge that she felt almost obliged to get Mr Kulkarni relieved of his concern for Kajal's future.

'Even without thinking of Papa, I gave Makrand's proposal serious thought. He has always come across as a very generous and understanding person, though, I do admit that I don't know him all that well,' Kajal explained to me. We were sitting in the spacious, high ceiling dining hall of our company club, the very evening when I returned to Jamshedpur.

'Then what did you decide? It seems from your tenor that you refused his proposal,' I said, masking my eagerness to hear her say the same.

'I talked to my father. I am rather fortunate to have such an understanding father. Love and understanding are two different things, and one does not necessarily lead to the other. Finally, I decided that I would not be happy living abroad, away from my country, family, and people.

It didn't feel fair to tell Makrand that, as he would perhaps have changed his life and returned to India for me. I wouldn't have liked that. I don't think my feelings for him deserve so much,' Kajal replied, looking out of the open window at the street full of blooming gulmohur and amaltash trees.

I hesitated about telling her about Riya. The vacillation between friendship and formality always remained with me. Till then I hadn't opened up to anyone about that morning with Riya. But I felt that not telling Kajal would be like concealing something from her, although she had never asked about me and Riya, and we seldom talked about that as if it didn't matter, as far as we were concerned. It had been as if Riya and I inhabited another planet, separate from the one that Kajal and I knew and lived on. But that other planet had moved away and disappeared, and I felt obliged to let Kajal know. If only because I knew that she was concerned about me and had expressed so.

'Riya and I have broken up. She decided that she can't come back to India,' I said.

I didn't want to use the cliché about 'breaking up' but couldn't find any other suitable phrase at that moment. I felt immediately that the explanation was both incomplete and unnecessary but there it was, out in the open.

Kajal looked up at my face, her eyes betraying her concern, looking for any signs of my feelings that would tell her the state of my mind. I don't think there was any. Whether she was relieved or puzzled, I can't say. We sat in silence, sipping at our lukewarm milky coffee from china cups bearing the company emblem on them.

'So? Do you want to talk about it?' Kajal asked after a

while. I had thought there was nothing much to talk about but still I spoke. But I found myself speaking about that evening twilight in the park rather than about the morning at Nirula's. I spoke about my present, future, and my life ahead as I saw it. I never realized when Kajal quietly had ordered for dinner, without interrupting my train of thought as they gushed forth.

'What do you say?' I asked her after sometime. 'You have not spoken.'

She quietly smiled. After all, I had hardly given her any chance to speak.

'Nirmaladi would be the happiest. And Vandana and others. Father too, I am sure. What does your family say?' she counter-questioned me, quietly side-stepping from what she herself felt. But I thought I knew.

'You are the first person to whom I have spoken about this,' I replied. Did that signify anything? Did I mean to signify anything?

'But I am sure they would be happy if they know I am happy,' I added.

'And I presume that you are not really heart-broken?' Kajal asked. 'I feared you would be.'

'I thought so too. But it is not as bad as I had imagined. I feel as if a heavy stone has been lifted from my chest and I am ready to breathe again. I had virtually forgotten to take a deep breath of fresh clean air,' I replied. 'As if a storm has cleared the sky and there is a distant light in the horizon,' I said.

Maybe, my expansive mood was making me lapse into poetry but Kajal didn't stop me. Poetry is after all not such a bad thing.

'So, tomorrow is a bright new day. Let us promise that every day would be new and bright, and we would be brave. I am happy for you and I am happy that you felt like sharing all this with me,' Kajal said, looking straight into my eyes. It was an honest, open look that didn't bother to conceal anything. She never had the vacillation between friendship and formality.

An almost full moon arose in the blue-black sky outside and we could both see the distant, but clear, milky glow that surrounded the moon. There were no clouds in the sky and silent music wafted across.

The night was indeed beautiful, but I was looking forward to the morning too.